Your Freshman Is Off To College

Your Freshman Is Off To College

A MONTH-BY-MONTH GUIDE
TO THE FIRST YEAR

● ● ●

Laurie L. Hazard, Ed.D.
& Stephanie K. Carter, M.A.

ISBN-13: 9781537682341
ISBN-10: 1537682342

Dedication

This book is dedicated to parents of first-year college students, who have tirelessly supported their children, from pre-school through high school, on their journey to higher education. We recognize the challenges of your evolving relationships with them and hope that this manual will provide insights to make this leg of the journey smoother.

Acknowledgements

● ● ●

THIS BOOK PROJECT HAS BEEN a "labor of love" over the last eight years. We have many people to thank for their help along the way.

Thanks to all of our friends and family who have encouraged us to write this book and have shared our enthusiasm for the project. Your support is greatly appreciated. We would also like to thank our Bryant University colleagues for what we have learned from collaborating with them on their work with parents and students through the years.

Thank you to Laura Kohl, Krystal Ristaino, and Shannon McAloon Merkler for their positive affirmations of our work and their invaluable feedback. A special thanks to our students, Kayla Navarro and Stephanie Leach, who offered their unique perspectives to ensure our book resonates with their generation. Toby Simon provided crucial insights into a particularly difficult topic for parents of first-year students; she has been a wonderful friend and mentor.

Thanks to Valerie Kisiel and Erin Hoag at Innovative Educators, who have included us on their journey of finding creative ways to communicate with students and their parents.

We are also appreciative of our partners at College Ready Parent™, Amy Baldwin and Brian Tietje, who have shared their vision and been generous with their expertise.

Finally, we are so grateful to our children, Grace, Jack, Sophie and Sarah, and our significant others, Stephen and Stephen, who have put up with our countless hours of discussing, writing and laughing through the years of this project.

About the Authors

LAURIE L. HAZARD IS THE Assistant Dean for Student Success at Bryant University in Smithfield, RI. As a member of the Applied Psychology Department, she writes about student personality types and classroom success. She is an award-winning expert on how students can make successful transitions from high school to college. After earning her Master's of Education degree from Boston University in counseling, she received a Doctoral degree from Boston University in Curriculum and Teaching. Laurie is co-author of the book *Foundations for Learning*, 3rd Edition (2012, Prentice Hall), which is designed to help students make a successful transition to college by encouraging them to take responsibility for and claim their own education. Hazard's textbook has been adopted by colleges and universities around the country, including Boston University, University of Nevada, and Texas A&M. Richard J. Light, the Walter H. Gale Professor of Education at Harvard University, calls Hazard's book "a winner for any college student" that is a "beautifully written joy to read."

Laurie has won numerous awards for her work with first-year students and their parents, including the National Resource Center for The First-Year Experience and Students in Transition's Outstanding First-Year Student Advocate; the Learning Assistance Association of New England's Outstanding Research and Publication Award; and the Learning Assistance Association of New England's Outstanding Service to Developmental

Students Award. Most recently, Laurie received the CRLA Northeast's Outstanding Service to the Field of Developmental Education Award.

Laurie's expertise has garnered national media attention. She has been interviewed and cited as an expert in the Associated Press, Seventeen Magazine, The Chicago Tribune, The Times Picayune, The San Diego Tribune, and Student Affairs Leader. Laurie has also been a guest columnist for the Washington Post's Answer Sheet: A School Survival Guide for Parents (And Everyone Else). Her articles offer concrete advice for parents of new college students: "How to Help Your Child Adapt to College Life," and "Parents Should Leave their Kids Alone at College." Laurie lives in Warwick, RI with her children Grace and Jack.

Stephanie Carter is the Director of the Academic Center for Excellence at Bryant University in Smithfield, Rhode Island. She is a respected leader in the field of student success and learning assistance. As an award-winning educator with over twenty-five years of experience helping college students mediate the challenges of the higher education environment, she has gained expertise working with first-years and their parents to insure a healthy transition from high school to college. Stephanie has extensive experience, as both a scholar and practitioner, supporting first-year college students in classrooms, residence halls, writing centers and learning centers. Stephanie earned her Master's degree in English at the University of Rhode Island. At Bryant University, Stephanie has developed curriculum for writing courses and teaches composition. She is a nationally recognized expert in the areas of plagiarism and academic integrity, as well as information literacy in the writing classroom. She is often an invited presenter for professional and faculty development in-services as well as for student programs. Stephanie lives in Warwick, RI with her husband Steve and her children, Sophie and Sarah.

Table of Contents

From The Point of ~~Conception~~ Acceptance

● ● ●

IT SEEMS JUST LIKE YESTERDAY when the stork landed to drop off that little bundle of joy in your nest. Your days, all those years ago, were filled with so many questions, "What should I do when my baby wakes up in the middle of the night? Run to the crib and pick her up? Let her cry it out? *If I only had a foolproof manual.* What should I feed my baby? Is organic baby food really that much better? *Aargh! I wish somebody would tell me what to do.* When will my baby crawl? Walk? Run? Shouldn't she be walking by now? *Please, someone tell me exactly what to expect!!!!!*"

Well, now your little ones are about to leave the nest. They have been accepted to college. Chances are, the days ahead will be filled with oh so many questions: "What should I do when my baby is homesick? Should I let her come back for a weekend? What should I do when my baby says the food at the dining hall sucks and she is starving to death? How is my baby surviving through her first months in college? Is she up and running? Will she make it to the finish line?" Well, guess what, empty nesters? You finally have that long awaited foolproof manual to answer these, and many more, questions about what you, as parents, should expect from your baby's first year of college.

This comprehensive guide is designed to assist you to support your young adult through the triumphs and pitfalls of their first year of college. The intention of the guide is not only to help you understand what to expect from your young adult as they walk through their first year of college, but also to provide you with some insight into what your young adult is likely experiencing during the course of that first-year. This insight will enable you to know *when* to step in and "baby" them, if necessary, and *when* to let go and allow them the freedom to learn from their mistakes. In short, this guide will assist you in supporting your young adult to have a successful first year. Let's face it: for you and your young adult, a lot is at stake.

Parents and students alike believe in the value of earning a college degree. Students believe that earning a college degree will help prepare them for a future career, while parents hope that a college diploma will secure better lives for their children (Boyer, 1987). Indeed, you're hoping that your young adults will be successful in college in order to secure jobs for themselves upon graduation, since college is a huge financial investment. Still, the transition from high school can cause a lot of angst, since many obstacles may get in the way as the dream of a degree becomes a reality. Fortunately, there is a lot that you, as parents, can do to help your young adults stay on track, dream big, and achieve their goals.

This stage of your young adult's life is one of the trickiest, though. Your job this year is to support them, not only in their transition from high school to college, but also in the process of moving out of the adolescent stage of development and into young adulthood. You will be challenged to figure out when to step in to help remove the obstacles that are impeding certain goals, and when to just plain old "let go" and allow your babies to stand on their own two feet, taking those wobbly steps toward full-fledged adulthood. This guide will help you figure out when to "let go of their hands."

Those wobbly steps toward full-fledged adulthood is unique to each individual. Some students will crawl through their first year, perhaps with less-than-desirable results. After the long nine months, many more will walk steadily to May's finish line earning solid grades. A few will run through the first year, returning as sophomores with an admirable cumulative grade point average, having made the dean's list not only one semester, but both their first year. What exactly should you expect from your young adult?

Although your little darling is certainly special, researchers and practitioners in higher education have identified some distinct patterns of experiences that your young adult will encounter in this developmental stage. Researchers have identified some distinct patterns of experiences that your young adult will encounter in this developmental stage. During the college years, students develop their intellectual capabilities and their sense of integrity. They move away from their parents' expectations as they establish their own identities. Emotionally, they learn how to create meaningful relationships and how to better understand their own feelings. Most importantly, at this stage, they figure out their own life's purpose and become independent adults.

How will all of this be accomplished, you ask? Well, it begins with the first year.

Practically speaking, first-year students will be challenged to establish future goals, get good grades, manage their time without your help or the assistance of a high school teacher, make friends, live on their own, and establish their identity, all the while attempting to be physically and emotionally healthy. Sound hard? Yup, growing up is hard to do. Luckily, you are here to support them through yet another developmental stage and this guide is thoughtfully designed to help you do just that.

CHAPTER FORMAT
UNCENSORED LETTER

Each chapter provides you with a month-by-month chronicle of the "first-year gestation period." Opening with an **Uncensored Letter** to parents, the purpose is to provide you with the inside track to what's going on with your babies, if only they could talk! The letter will introduce you to a variety of typical obstacles, challenges or issues that your young adults may face in that particular month. Many times, college students are afraid to tell mom and dad exactly what's going on. You have such high expectations for them that first year, and they don't want to feel like they are letting you down. The letter will not only give you the inside track, but it will also provide you with some clues as to what more to ask about if your young adults call and merely hint at some of these issues. They just might not have the vocabulary yet to explain the whole story! You will need to help them along.

Growing Pains: What Your ~~Baby~~ Young Adult May Experience This Month

As mentioned, for most students, the transition from high school to college lasts nearly the whole first year and follows a distinct developmental pattern. Each month is marked by typical developmental challenges. For instance, if your young adult is living away at college, it is typical that they may experience some degree of homesickness in the first month. Remember when they moved out of the crib into the "big kids' bed?" Some babies adjust very quickly to the new sleeping arrangement with little disruption of their sleep patterns, while others take a lot longer to get used to the idea of sleeping without the safety of the crib and its bumpers. Should you put up a guard rail? You will have many questions about what to do to help your young adult through all of these new situations. Knowing that all college students are, to some degree, adjusting to their new surroundings, each chapter has a list of patterned experiences that your young adults will face during the months ahead called **Growing Pains: What Your ~~Baby~~ Young Adult May Experience This Month.**

Your Questions, Our Answers, and Setting Expectations

What to do? What to do? So many questions.............not to worry. Each chapter contains a variety of typical questions you will have related to the monthly milestones. Answers are provided by practitioners in the family practice of Hazard and Carter – experts on adolescent development and the transition from high school to college. With the idea of letting go of your baby's hand, each answer not only gives you solid advice about how to handle the given situation, but also offers concrete directions for exactly what your young adult should do in this situation. In other words, this part of the chapter tells you what to expect in a particular month and, at the same time, helps you set expectations for your young adult. Aptly titled, **What to expect of your ~~baby~~ young adult in this situation,** this section gives you a vehicle to impart concrete practical advice of what type of action your baby should take, and how you should follow up.

STEP-BY-STEP . . .

Each chapter has advice about college and university resources entitled **Step-By-Step . . .** The purpose is to point your young adult in the direction of a particular campus department whose function it is to help your child deal with the challenges that they may be facing. For instance, your son's roommate constantly allows his girlfriend to sleep over and it is creating a very awkward situation. Your son calls you and says, "I can't take this anymore!" Do you step in to help? That is, do you contact the Office of Residence Life for him? Oh no, you don't. He does. So, then what do you do? Explain that there is a campus resource that can assist him. Send him there and, at a later agreed upon date, check to see if he followed through on his own. Let the steps toward independence and young adulthood begin.

For most, this transition from adolescence to young adulthood begins in the summer months, when your baby is preparing to leave the nest. So, the first chapter picks up there.

CHAPTER 1

Preparing for Delivery: Summer

● ● ●

PARENTS, WHEN YOUR CHILDREN WERE babies, you likely experienced mixed emotions as they reached and surpassed each precious developmental milestone. You couldn't wait for them to be finished with bottles and onto eating solid food. You were dying for them to get out of diapers and to potty training. Remember wishing for the day when they finally would enroll in school full-time? Although you may have fantasized about the future when they would be through these challenging stages, at the same time, you probably had mixed emotions - you certainly didn't want to wish those treasured years away. In just a few short weeks now, they will be in school full-time, possibly living away from you . . . some of them pretty far. For both you and your young adult, the days preceding the delivery date to college are indeed filled with mixed emotions.

For you moms and dads, there's the excitement about turning that bedroom into a nice workout room, state-of-the-art media room, or comfortable new study, yet you are worried about what it's going to be like not knowing exactly what time your baby drifts off to sleep. Your young adults are anticipating their upcoming freedom with unbridled enthusiasm, similar to the days when they were determined to climb out of their cribs. You've heard it, "I can't wait to get out of here." You're thinking, "If only they knew what I know now............." Freedom is not all that it's cracked up to be, right? Wait until they have to do all their own laundry and when they reach for the detergent, it's not there. Who buys it now?

At the moment, you are observing the all too familiar adolescent bravado, the thrill of high school graduation, and the high of the

1

accomplishment of college acceptance. You are watching the beginnings of the "honeymoon stage," if you will, of the transition between adolescence and young adulthood. Underneath it all, they actually may be worried about making friends and concerned about missing you, siblings, friends, and perhaps even a family pet. They even may be wondering if they have what it takes to make it academically in college. They may not let you see what's really going on inside. Well, there is good news and bad news. The good news is that most colleges and universities have "birthing class" to help you and your babies sort through these mixed emotions and prepare for the looming delivery date. The bad news is, you are likely more ready to hear what the "birthing classes" have to say than your babies are.

BIRTHING CLASSES: NEW STUDENT ORIENTATION

Unlike the birthing class that you and your partners attended in preparation for the arrival of your little darlings, birthing classes in higher education are usually a family affair. That's right: many colleges offer birthing classes for both parents and first-year students. These classes usually are called something like "New Student Orientation." Orientations typically take place sometime in June or July before your babies' official delivery date to the institution, which likely will be sometime toward the middle or end of August.

For your babies, orientation is designed to acclimate them to their new cribs. You will drop them off with a babysitter: yup, someone not much older than they are who recently passed through this developmental stage. These babysitters may be called orientation leaders. The orientation leaders will hold their hands through the birthing class activities that will cover a variety of relatively standard topics:

- Learning about majors and minors offered at the institution in more depth.
- Getting to know their "babysitters" and "new playmates" a little better.

- Finding out about special programs such as honors programs or study abroad opportunities.
- Understanding what it's going to be like to live in the residence hall or commute to the institution.
- Taking placement exams in math, English, and foreign languages.
- Becoming familiar with the campus climate by attending discussions on drug and alcohol usage, sexuality, personal wellness, and diversity to name a few.
- Registering for fall classes.
- Meeting faculty, advisors, and other key personnel at the institution like the dean, or perhaps even the president.
- Gaining insight into the importance of campus involvement.
- Gathering information about the location of important offices and services such as financial aid, the library, and campus technology resources.
- Learning where to go if all of this seems too overwhelming: academic services such as tutoring, academic advising, and personal counseling.

All of this sounds incredibly informative, doesn't it? How great it is that institutions of higher education offer such comprehensive birthing classes before your babies even start. What more will your babies/young adults need? Let's see . . . . . remember when your little ones were learning to walk and got over-stimulated by the novel discoveries from their new vantage point? When attention could not be focused on one thing for very long periods? At that time, so much in your babies' environment was new; it was overwhelming. Well, during orientation, the same thing is happening all over again.

At orientation, first-year students are inundated with so much new information, it can be overwhelming. To make matters worse, right now, concerns are centered around "who is hot, and who is not," who will sit with them in the cafeteria, who will end up in the playpen with them, and who will be "friended" on Facebook or "followed" on Instagram after orientation ends. At the moment, they are not incredibly tuned into the fact that the institution has an Office of Career Services that can help them polish their interviewing skills when it comes time to apply for a job. That's the bad news. Chances are, they are not paying attention to all of this wonderful information as you would like them to; in short, they are on information overload.

The good news is that many colleges and universities have birthing classes designed for parents, too. Parent classes usually take place simultaneously to your sons' and daughters', pretty much covering the same topics, but with a different audience in mind: you. So parents and guardians, you have a job to do. Pay attention. Gather as much information at orientation as you possibly can. On the ride home, bring up some of the topics that were covered to see how much your young adult remembers. Share with them what you found to be most informative or interesting. If your babies are exhausted, and don't seem to want to engage in the discussion, not to worry; you have the information when they are ready to hear it. Armed with that, you have the ability to point them in the right direction whenever they need it.

MATERNITY AND PATERNITY LEAVE

Once the August delivery date rolls around, you will be dropping your babies off at college. Unlike your last maternity or paternity leave, you will not be taking your little ones home with you. That's right. "Move-In Day" at colleges and universities nationwide give a whole new meaning to parental leave. You got it. Personnel in higher education want you to deliver your babies and leave! Don't call. Don't e-mail. Don't text, at least for a few days. How about waiting until they call you? Let go of their hands. Let them take those wobbly first steps toward young adulthood. Try not to worry too much, most colleges and universities have ample programming to help pick them up if they fall. Why is it that institutions of higher education don't want you involved?

Hmmmmm . . . . . how to say this gently? You are a generation of parents heavily involved in your babies' lives. Perhaps too involved. In fact, our popular culture has a name for you: *helicopter parents.* Why helicopter parents? Well, you hover over your young adults, "flooding campus orientations, meddling in registration and interfering with their dealings with professors, administrators, and roommates" (Shellenbarger, 2005). This hovering "undermines non-classroom lessons on problem solving, seeking help, and compromising what should be part of a college education" (Pope, 2005). Some higher education experts even believe that you are stunting their growth and undermining their success. We know that's certainly not what you want for your young adults.

That's why birthing classes are offered - to help you strike a balance, and so too will this instruction manual. Remember, it's time for you to let your babies grow up. Adam Weinberg, a dean at Colgate University, sums it up quite well. He basically says that your babies should leave the nursery and become functioning, autonomous people (Weinberg, as cited in Pope, 2005). That's what college is for: let them take those wobbly steps toward adulthood - alone. Okay, okay . . . not quite so alone. That is, it is now time for them to learn about the myriad programs in higher education designed to take them from walking to running. Let them learn about these support systems first-hand, experiencing them with the help of the experts-on campus.

Support Away From Home

Though you are not leaving your babies alone in the woods with the big bad wolf, you are still very worried. According to the Second Annual Survey on College Parent Experiences (2007), health and safety concerns rank second to concerns about finances. Academics rank third on your list of fears. Guess what? Your young adult will have a residential support system to watch over them after you drop them off.

Resident Assistants, called RAs, provide live-in support for your young adult. RAs are students, usually undergraduates, who have taken on a helping role in the residence hall. They live in close proximity to your sons and daughters and are there to help them with a wide variety of issues such as roommate conflicts, homesickness, and health and safety concerns, to name a few. You will learn more about the duties of the RA in upcoming chapters.

Additional support will come from a variety of university administrators and faculty, including a first-year experience[1] (FYE) course instructor. FYE course instructors may take the lead in helping your young adult with the transition from high school to college. According to a national survey, some 80% of colleges and universities offer a first-year experience or first-year seminar classes. Though the purposes, names, formats, and numbers of credits offered, vary widely across institutions of higher education, the fact remains that the majority of colleges and universities offer some type of course to help your sons and daughters acclimate to their new crib.

Regardless of the differences, there are some objectives and topics that are standard in such courses. The three most common objectives are to develop academic skills, provide information on campus resources and services, and encourage self-exploration and personal development. Common topics include: study skills, campus resources, time management, academic planning, and critical thinking. Exactly what your young adults need, right? If you were concerned that they didn't pay attention at orientation, the first-year class will remind them of what's available as they need it, as the semester unfolds. Once again though, you are probably more enthusiastic about them taking this course than they are. Why is that?

Well, let's face it. They are still teetering in the adolescent stage of development. They already know everything, right? What could you or colleges and universities possibly say to them about managing their time? After all, they have had all sorts of electronic devices since they were, well, babies. So, what do you say to them when they call, and say, "I have this stupid course that's a waste of time! This week we are talking about time management......argh. Like I don't know how to manage my time!"?

---

1 The concept of a First-Year Experience course was first developed by John N. Gardner in 1986. John Gardner founded The National Resource Center which disseminates information on the First-Year Experience through scholarly publications, and national and international conferences. For more information, see the website for The National Resource Center at http://sc.edu/fye/

How do you respond? Have a conversation that goes something like this, encouraging your sons and daughters to be open to the new information and experiences:

concrete examples

Mom:	I've got a great analogy for you. How do you lose weight?
Daughter:	I dunno Get on the treadmill and reduce your calories?
Mom:	Uh huh. Do you think your father knows how to lose weight, and isn't he always trying?
Daughter:	Yeah... so?
Mom:	Well if he knows how to lose weight, then why does he still have a huge Buddha belly?!

You may grant to your sons and daughters that they may "already know" some of the content of the first-year transition courses, and they may; however, the point of these courses is not simply to teach them how to "manage time" or "take notes," for example. Rather, these courses are designed to motivate them to actually *apply* some of the skills and strategies that are being taught to them. That is, those strategies that will help them be more successful students.

Most of us indeed do know how much sleep we need, how to eat healthy, and how to manage our time, but there can be many obstacles that get in the way, and derail us, thus preventing us from reaching our goals. So, most first-year courses have a higher purpose beyond educating your sons and daughters about campus resources. These courses, if they are designed well, focus on the psychological aspects of adjusting to college.

Let's say your son or daughter is having difficulty in math during the first semester. What you want them to DO is seek out tutoring. They THINK tutoring won't help; they FEEL embarrassed about getting a tutor because they always did well in math in high school, and their attitude is, "Why should I bother; it won't help anyway." Your job, in addition to the goal of these courses, is to help them overcome the self-defeating thoughts and attitudes, so they DO what will help them to be successful in college.

What each student needs to do to be successful varies widely, as students come from diverse backgrounds, experiences, and levels of preparation, so

growth mindset

the contents of these courses vary to meet the individual needs of your oh-so-special babies. If your young adult is willing to be open to the experience, there is something in these courses for every first-year student.

For example, students who are resistant to tutoring are often the ones struggling with academic adjustment issues. Those same students may have no trouble at all making friends and joining clubs or organizations. For them, the social adjustment is a piece of cake. Adjustment challenges in college may be academic, social, intellectual or emotional. Emotional adjustment may include struggles with homesickness, such as missing a younger sibling, grandparent, or even a pet. For young adults, intellectual adjustment may come in the form of finding out that their political views drastically diverge from their political science professor, for instance. How will they reconcile this?

Simple: ask their first-year experience instructor for help. First-year experience instructors have the expertise to assist your sons and daughters with the myriad of adjustment issues they may face during the first year. Whether the adjustment challenges are intellectual, emotional, academic, or social, the FYE instructor is equipped to help.

What can you do? Well, as mentioned, the extent to which particular adjustment topics are covered varies among institutions and their course curricula. Your job is to ask the right questions when your sons and daughters call with complaints, concerns, and challenges. In the upcoming months, we will show you how to do that. Your job is to help your children figure out what they need and support them, FROM A DISTANCE, through the college adjustment. Of course, this manual is here to help you.

Developing Habits of Mind for Success in College and Life (Hazard and Nadeau, 2012)

Remember in kindergarten when you hoped that your little ones would learn their manners, and actually use them when you were not around? You prayed that they didn't behave like animals in the absence of your close monitoring? You cringed when they didn't say please and thank you? At that time, you worked diligently encouraging your sons and daughters to use their manners and develop good habits. Well, we want what you want for your babies.

The goal of this manual is to help you help your sons and daughters continue to develop habits of mind that will enable them to be successful in college and in life. So, if they do complain about that first-year experience class and their college experience in general, gently remind them that the objective of that class and one of the goals of higher education itself holds a higher purpose for them-to develop lifetime habits, which will enable their success and happiness.

In the months ahead, you will come to understand the obstacles and challenges that your sons and daughters will face. If they learn (what they tell you they "already know" as they roll their eyes at you) and actually apply (that's the key!) some of these habits as they traverse their first year of college, they will be prepared for their futures. For instance, if they say, "Why do I have to read *Romeo and Juliet* again? I read it in the ninth grade!!!!" You'll say, "Well dear, you are an English literature major and you did register for a Survey of Shakespeare class. In college, you will likely get into a more in-depth analysis of the characters and plot of this classic. In fact, some people choose to earn their master's degrees in Shakespearean literature. I am guessing you don't know EVERYTHING about *Romeo and Juliet*. Be open to learning something new." In other words, moms and dads, teach your babies that those who **possess humility** are more likely to be successful; developing this disposition will make for a more positive experience.

Having the ability to **ask for help** is another habit that is critical to college success. There will be countless times where your sons and daughters will have to ask a faculty member, a tutor, a resident assistant, a coach, or a friend for help. Encourage them that this is OK. Asking for help is not a sign of weakness; rather, it is an indication that they are mature enough to recognize their strengths and challenges (as we all have them) and are **taking responsibility** to gain control of their situation. To that end, they must be **willing to change**. Let's say they recognize that they are struggling with the format of multiple- choice exams. Their FYE instructor recommends that they go to the university's tutoring center for help, and so they go. The professional staff member there points out that it's the particular study strategy they are using that is holding them back. That person implores them to change and try a new strategy. For some students, trying a new study strategy that is out of their comfort zone is hard. Encourage them to take a leap of faith. That is, take risks. Research shows that the same study habits that helped students succeed in high school are unrelated to college performance (Matt et al., 1991); therefore, it is inevitable that your babies/young adults will have to change at least some of their study habits.

Taking calculated risks is part of the college (and life) experience. Your role is to be there to support and encourage your sons and daughters through this major life transition (albeit from a distance). Don't be afraid to ask for help. This manual is here not only to help you do that, but also to support you in your major life transition: evolving from being parents of adolescents into being parents of adults (yes, that's right).

Rest assured, the majority of first-year students have a healthy, successful first year and adjust to the pitfalls and challenges of college life. But unfortunately, sexual assault is a serious problem on college campuses, and we would be remiss if we did not address this important topic at the outset of discussing your young adult's first-year experience.

A Word or Two about Sexual Assault on Campus

Toby Simon, Former Vice President of Student Affairs, Marymount Manhattan College and Associate Dean of Student Life, Brown University

Wouldn't it be nice if we didn't need to include this topic in a "how-to" manual for parents sending their young adult off to college? But we do and here's why: studies show that the most vulnerable time for first-year women to be sexually assaulted on campus is during their first three months on campus. Living away from home for the first time, new independence, wanting to fit in with others, alcohol and drug availability, and alcohol use and misuse are among the reasons cited for this increased vulnerability.

And nothing can be more traumatizing, destabilizing and ruinous of a college experience than to be a victim of sexual violence. The same can be said for a student accused of sexually assaulting a peer.

The good news is that now, more than ever before, campus sexual assaults are receiving national attention. Colleges have to be much more vigilant with their reporting of incidents, providing information on procedures and policies to address allegations of sexual violence, and conducting prevention and education programs during orientation programs and throughout the year. Thanks to Title IX legislation, colleges must adhere to specific policies on sexual assault or risk losing federal funding should they be in violation of the law.

Although there are now over 200 US colleges in violation of the Title IX regulations, the majority of these schools are responding to the requirements to rectify their situations. And now every university is required to comply with the regulations. For your son or daughter, this means that they will be learning more about sexual assault in their first few weeks on campus than they did while in high school.

These educational programs also include information about how to report a sexual assault, where to find the women's advocates on and off campus, and important issues on confidentiality. Schools often use peers to deliver the important messages about consent, alcohol, and sexual communications. Many programs now include bystander education, which empowers peers to intervene if they see something that may be problematic. The message is that peers have the power to stop sexual assaults from ever happening if they are aware of the potential disaster. They have the power to choose to stop the offending behavior or help the potential victim get out of a dangerous situation.

In my 35 years of experience working with college women (and sometimes men) who were sexually assaulted, they were often reluctant to tell their parents about the assault. Although I encouraged with these students to figure out a way to tell mom or dad what happened, sometimes they just couldn't do it and in my role as a university administrator, I was bound to protect their confidentiality. This is an unbearable pill to swallow for many parents who really want to help and support their daughter in the event of an assault. This is why it may be extremely useful to convey to your about- to- start- college adolescent, that you understand sexual assault is a real concern on every college campus and that if anything like that ever happened to them or a friend, you would want to know and you would unequivocally support them. You can convey that you understand that sometimes people in college drink too much and/or put themselves in dangerous situations. In the event of a sexual assault, these are important messages to stress, even if you might actually be disappointed or angry with your daughter. She likely feels awful enough. You can remind her that bad judgement is not a rape-able offense.

There's way too much at stake for young adults new to a college community to be either the victim or perpetrator of a sexual assault. Fortunately, realistic programs that combine education on sexuality and alcohol use, along with competent college personnel to help students, and strong university policies about zero tolerance for sexual assault, all greatly improve the college climate and ultimately reduce the incidence of sexual violence on campus.

CHAPTER 2

September

● ● ●

September 15

Dear Mom,

I WANT TO COME HOME! I had no idea how different college would be from high school. Everyone here is so weird compared to the kids at home. My roommate is OK, but it's hard to know who to be friends with here. Friday night, a bunch of girls from my floor invited me to go with them to a party, but I barely knew them, and being at a party with them was strange. Amy ended up getting so drunk that she threw up all over the place and I had to drag her home. Jessica hooked up with some guy she just met, and I didn't see her again until lunch the next day! When I asked her how she got home, she said she didn't even remember! Who are these girls? I need to find people more like my friends from home.

My classes are so different from high school, too. The teachers are so intimidating. They expect us to know everything - they don't even tell us what's for homework. In history class the other day, my professor gave a quiz that everyone else seemed ready for, except me. I asked the kid next to me about it. He just said that the quiz was mentioned on the syllabus. How was I supposed to know that?! I'm gonna flunk out of here!

When can you come get me?

Love,
Emily

Growing Pains: What May Be Causing Your ~~Baby's~~ Young Adult's Stranger Anxiety This Month

- Learning how to live with a roommate (or multiple roommates)
- Navigating the college campus (and probably getting lost once or twice)
- Getting a taste of freedom: having too much time with not enough structure on how to spend it, and no one to tell them to do their homework, to wake up, or be home by curfew
- Attending parties, complete with drinking and hooking up
- Wondering if they can handle the academic challenges
- Trying to find friends to sit with at dinner, to study with, and to hang out with on weekends
- Finding new ways to handle (and spend) money
- Dealing with homesickness and missing family, friends, boyfriends, girlfriends
- Experiencing a crisis of values as many of their beliefs will be challenged by meeting new people and encountering new experiences

ROOMMATE PROBLEMS

My son is complaining about his roommate, Andrew. He says that Andrew is a slob and is up all night. He can't stand him. What can he do? What can I do to help?

Just as your son had to learn to share toys in preschool, now he has to learn to share space with a roommate. When you talk to your son, you can suggest a few ways he can handle this situation with his roommate. First, encourage your son to make an effort to get to know his roommate a little bit better. It's easier to negotiate with someone if you understand where they are coming from. Even though he might not be crazy about spending MORE time with his roommate, he could invite him to join him for dinner or to study together for an hour at the library. Once a better rapport has been established, it might be easier for your son to say, "Dude, could you keep your dirty clothes in a laundry bag please?" and it's more likely to bring out a better response from his roommate.

If your son can't improve his relationship with his roommate after a few attempts, they still might be able to find a way to live together peacefully. Roommates don't have to be best friends, but they do need to be able to treat each other respectfully, so that both feel comfortable spending time in their room, their "home away from home." Your son may need to start a conversation with Andrew about some "rules of the room". As hard as it may be to believe, Andrew may have problems with some of your son's habits, too! They should try to talk about ways to handle certain situations (like using headphones to listen to music after 11 pm). Encourage your son to avoid getting defensive in his conversation with Andrew, and to be willing to change some of his own behaviors as well. Give something to get something.

It may turn out that your son is not able to resolve the situation himself without any outside help. There are campus resources that can help with these types of roommate problems. Each resident is assigned a **resident assistant** (recall that live-in "nanny," usually called an **RA** at most universities). Most RAs have some training in roommate conflict resolution, and can help mediate with both parties or refer students to someone who can. In these types of mediations, both roommates can negotiate room rules, and agree to abide by them.

If mediation does not help your son reach a solution with his roommate, it may be time for him to consider changing rooms. Each residential university has a **department of residential life** (or the equivalent). The people in this department may be able to help your son find a new roommate. If the situation gets to this point for your son, you may need to help your son weigh the pros and cons of changing roommates. For instance, your son may need to move to a new residence hall, further from some of his current friends. On the other hand, he may be able to move to a residence hall that is closer to some of his classes, for example. You can help him deliberate about whether he'd rather stick it out for the year. He'll then have more control over his living situation in his sophomore year in college, when students typically choose their own roommates, rather than having one assigned.

What to expect of your ~~baby~~ young adult in this situation:

- Make some attempts to get to know his roommate a little better.
- Talk to his roommate about settling on some rules that they can both live with.
- If attempts to talk to his roommate don't succeed, he will then talk to his RA about the situation.
- If the RA can't help him and his roommate resolve their problems, he will then go to the residential life office to talk about rooming options, and possibly changing rooms.

[handwritten: Step-by-step ideas]

Dealing With Privacy Issues

My daughter is an only child. She has never had to worry about sharing a room with someone and has always relished her privacy. She is complaining about how weird it is to have her roommate come in and out of the room without knocking. She is just so modest; it is embarrassing her to have to get dressed in front of her roommate. She told me her roommate just flings her clothes off, and parades around the room in her underwear. My daughter is mortified!

Perhaps one of the most difficult parts of the college transition for some students who choose to live on campus is getting used to sharing space with a roommate. For the most part, this person really is a total stranger (at first). Rest assured though, many first-year students who have chosen to live on campus survive those awkward first few weeks with a new roommate. They may even become great friends. As an only child, your daughter may need some additional adjustment time compared to students who come from homes with siblings and step-siblings.

What may be helpful is if your daughter and her roommate have a conversation regarding "house rules," if you will. That is, they may want to sit down together and brainstorm some basic "rules of the room" that they can both live with. Still, broaching a conversation addressing intimates like underwear can be a little awkward, even for the most self-assured adult.

Most would be apt to start out a conversation about such an issue like this, "You make me feel really strange when you walk around the room in your underwear. It's totally weird that you do that!!!" Starting out a conversation with "you" tends to put a person on the defensive. Rather, have her try a basic conflict resolution technique. Start out the conversation with "I." For instance, "I would like to talk to you about a concern of mine. I feel a little uncomfortable during the times you change your clothes, and when you hang out in the room in your underwear. I am wondering if you would consider wearing a robe or sweats instead." Using "I" statements allows your daughter to assume some of the responsibility in the situation. Both roommates have accountability for creating a comfortable climate in the room.

Still, the roommate in her underwear raises issues of privacy, and there are many other privacy issues to be considered, which is why roommates should have a "rules of the room" conversation early on. Roommates may overhear private conversations. With the ubiquitous use of Facetime, texting, and social media, like Facebook, has confidentiality been discussed? Each other's friends and partners will be coming in and out. Have appropriate quiet times in the room been established? Rules for having overnight guests? Clothes, computers, jewelry, and other belongings like IPads may be in the room. Is this a "what's yours is mine" situation, or will there be rules about what can be borrowed and when?

Chances are many of these issues have been addressed in orientation and during hall meetings. Resident Assistants and Directors usually conduct hall meetings once a month (more at the beginning for first-years) to address many of these and other similar issues. Some colleges even have roommates sign contracts agreeing to a set of rules. What typically happens though, if particular issues (like eating your roommate's food, for example) haven't cropped up at the times that the meetings take place, the suggestions for dealing with such situations might be ignored. You may have to step in and talk your young adult through how to handle new situations that may arise.

What to expect of your ~~baby~~ young adult in this situation:

* She will give it one more week without saying anything to see if the underwear parade is a fluke or a regular occurrence.
* If it becomes clear that it's a regular occurrence, she will try the conflict resolution technique and use it as an opportunity to have the "rules of the room" brainstorming session.
* If attempts to talk to her roommate don't succeed, then she will talk to her RA about the situation.
* If the RA can't help them resolve their problems, then she will go to the residential life office to talk about rooming options, and possibly changing rooms.

HANDLING NEW FREEDOMS

My daughter was really sheltered in high school. I'm worried about how she's handling all this freedom. When I talk to her, she sounds happy and says everything is fine, but it's so hard to know without seeing her face to face.

Remember when your daughter started crawling for the first time? At first it was great, and she probably was so excited to be able to get to wherever she wanted in the house, all by herself. But after a little while, it became clear that your baby needed some limits, and you put up baby gates around the house to keep her safe. Your daughter is again feeling excited about being independent; she needs to learn how to set her own boundaries and limits, now that she's in college and there are no baby gates around.

The sense of newfound freedom may be experienced in different areas of your daughter's life. Socially, first year students may go to parties and drink alcohol. For some first year students, this experimentation with alcohol started in high school, but for others, this may be the first time they have done so or even had any exposure to drinking. You can do very little about this, but try to get a sense of your daughter's new friends and her social activities.

If she is candid with you and tells you about drinking, you can use this as an opportunity to talk with her about your beliefs about alcohol consumption, and you can give her some ideas on how to be safe. At some universities, the **health services department** offers student education programs related to alcohol and drugs. Other campuses incorporate alcohol education as part of their student wellness programs. You can encourage your daughter to attend one of these programs. You should also make yourself and your daughter aware of the university's policy on underage drinking and the consequences for violating these policies. Violation penalties (often found in the student handbook), vary according to university, but can include mandatory education and community service programs, probation, expulsion from the residence hall, and expulsion from the university.

Another way that your daughter may be feeling the effects of freedom is in her academics. In college, most classes meet around three hours per week. So, if your daughter is taking five classes, she is in class for fifteen hours each week. Compare that to the thirty hours a week that most high school students spend in school, and it's clear that most college students have lots of unstructured time on their hands.

It's hard at first for first-year students to realize that college courses are really quite different from high school classes. They may still refer to their professors as teachers, and expect the faculty to be giving them reminders about due dates and quizzes. Instead, professors typically spell out the ways that their students should be using their time outside of class in a document called a syllabus. Faculty give students the syllabus during the first days of class, and expect the students to complete all the requirements laid out in it. They do not necessarily review the syllabus with the students, or remind them of what requirements are due. This puts a great deal of responsibility on the student. You can help your daughter by encouraging her to be organized for her academic work for the semester with a calendar. You can also stress to your daughter that she must set aside time to get her work done each day. She should be balancing her work in the classroom with additional hours on each course outside the classroom, and should be completing this work before any social activities.

Although she'll continue to experience her new sense of freedom, and will want to try new things over the next few weeks, at some point, she will need to find a balance between her course work and her leisure time. One of the best things you can do to help your daughter learn how to set her own limits is to keep communication open with her. Of course college and early adulthood is a time for our kids to test freedom and limits. These experiences will help them learn and mature. The values you have instilled in your daughter up to this point will hopefully stay with her as she's learning to set her own boundaries and limits.

What to expect of your ~~baby~~ young adult in this situation:

* She will talk to you about social activities that may be interfering with her academics.
* She will check the alcohol-related policies in her student handbook.
* She will review all of her syllabi closely and make note of all due dates and assignments in a calendar.
* She will talk to her professors if she has trouble with any of her courses.

Homesickness

My daughter has been very emotional during her phone calls home. She has only been away for one week, and she wants to plan on coming home for the next three weekends straight. She really seems to miss her sisters and her friends from high school, many of whom are living in our hometown still.

It's so hard not to run to the campus to scoop up your daughter and bring her home when she's feeling homesick. It's kind of like the first time you left your daughter at preschool. She may have cried and fussed the first time, which made it hard for both of you. But eventually, she became comfortable with her new surroundings, even if it wasn't quite as comfy as home. Homesickness is very common, and is part of the normal process for young adults away at college for the first time.

The tricky thing with homesickness is that the apparent cure, a visit home, can worsen the symptoms when your daughter returns to campus. Frequent visits home, particularly so early in the first semester, can prevent your daughter from making the new on-campus connections that would help her start to feel more comfortable while in college. This is because the majority of a university's recreational and social events happen on weekends. If everyone else was at the dance-athon over the weekend while she was away, your daughter is probably going to feel left out of the conversations and relationships created around this event. So, while everyone else (or what feels like everyone else) is getting to know one another and bonding, your daughter is with you and her old friends instead. This may give your daughter's new acquaintances and fledgling friends the sense that your daughter really isn't interested in building relationships at school.

So, the first step for you is to really encourage your daughter to stay on campus for the weekend. When your daughter asks you (or tells you) that she'd like to spend the weekend at home, resist the temptation to say, "Sure, honey. We've missed you, too!" Consider putting the brakes on her plans a bit. You could try saying "You are always welcome to come home, of course, but how about staying on campus this weekend, and why don't you come for a visit on the next long weekend instead?" If you wanted to take a harder line based on your style, you could even dictate how many weeks you expect her to stay on campus before coming home for a weekend.

If your daughter says something like "Everyone at home is getting together tomorrow night! What am I supposed to do here?", then try encouraging her to look into what's going on around campus. She could approach an acquaintance that lives on the same floor of her residence hall, or a friendly face from her math class, or her RA to find out how people are spending their weekend time. And hopefully, she'll get an invite or two in the process.

If your daughter has trouble putting herself out there and taking the initiative to make plans, she can still find a way to have a tolerable weekend on campus. Encourage her to get some homework done, to hang out in her residence hall's common room, and to get a better feel for her new home away from home. And who knows? She may end up getting an impromptu invitation for dinner and a movie with a bunch of the girls from her floor.

You can also help your daughter to move past her homesickness by talking to her about getting more actively involved on campus. Have this conversation early in the week, before the weekend ahead starts looming over her. There are many campus organizations and clubs that are available for all students to join. These clubs and groups are excellent cures for homesickness for a couple of reasons. First, lots of clubs schedule activities and events during the weekend, giving students things to do instead of going home. Second, clubs and organizations are a great way for your daughter to connect with other people who share her interests. She can find out more information about clubs and organizations on campus by visiting the **student activities office** or **student involvement office**.

So, if your daughter loves to write, she might want to join the student newspaper. She may then want to stay on campus to write a feature on the Saturday football game, while at the same time she gets the chance to hang out with all the other student-journalists who are trying to get the issue finished before the 11 PM deadline on Sunday.

If your daughter is really resisting the idea of staying at school for the weekend, you could try making a deal with her. For example, you could ask her to try to stay on campus for the next few weeks, with a promise that you'll pick her up for the Columbus Day weekend, and have her favorite lasagna waiting when she gets home. Or, maybe you could let her know that you and her sisters will come to visit her on campus one Saturday or Sunday instead of her coming home to you.

Also, encourage your daughter to speak with her **RA** about her feelings. RAs are an excellent resource for first year students. They know all about what is happening on campus, and, because they get to know all of their residents personally, they can also help forge friendships between the people on her floor. Your daughter's RA has received some training on how to help homesick students, and will be able to help with her adjustment.

Occasionally, homesickness can prevent young adults from being able to perform their schoolwork and enjoy their lives. If you feel like your daughter is depressed, or that her homesickness is preventing her from managing her coursework, it's time for a serious, face to face talk. It would be important to probe and find out exactly why your daughter is so unhappy at school.

Keep in mind that most universities have a **counseling office** staffed with mental health professionals. You can encourage your daughter to visit the counseling office and schedule an appointment to speak with someone who has experience dealing with college student homesickness. Together, they can work on strategies for making connections at school.

What to expect of your baby young adult in this situation:

* She will make an attempt to get to know people on campus, and to find out what activities are available on weekends.
* She will stay on campus most weekends, starting with this one.
* She will look for an activity, club or organization on campus that she would like to join.
* She will talk to her RA about feeling homesick.
* If she continues to experience homesickness, she will visit the counseling office and make use of its resources.

CULTURE SHOCK AND QUESTIONING VALUES

I'm getting the sense that my son is uneasy with the amount of "hooking up" going on among the young men and women at his school. We are a very religious family, and my son went to thirteen years of Catholic school. He's never really been exposed to this kind of behavior, and I think he's kind of shocked by it all.

Just like in the potty-training stage of development, the college student's focus may still be on the genitals, only for a whole different reason! Your son is getting a little taste of culture shock right now. The sometimes sexually-charged atmosphere of a college campus may be a drastic change from your son's high school experience. When you think of it, this atmosphere isn't really surprising, given that college students are relishing and testing their freedoms while simultaneously testing and trying to understand their system of values. Throw some hormones in there, and you've got a recipe for some wild nights.

Your son is probably observing all this, and wondering how his classmates' and dorm-mates' behaviors fit in with his own values. He might be questioning whether he can find true friends among people with such different values. Or maybe he's thinking, "Wait a minute – why is everyone else having so much more fun than I am?" This questioning and rethinking of one's values is normal and common during the first year of college, and is a key step in your son's emotional development.

So, how can you help your son in this process? One of the most important ways is to begin (or continue) an ongoing, casual dialogue about your morals, values, and faith, and how these are tested in all sorts of situations in life. Try to remain relatively neutral when he is telling you about the behaviors of others. If he tells you that his roommate had two different girls sleep over on two consecutive nights, try to refrain from expressing your shock or disgust. Instead, consider trying the old stand-by therapist question of "How did this make you feel?" Instead of making the judgment calls for him, let your son do the heavy lifting. Your son will be more likely to discuss matters with you if he's not afraid of horrifying you with stories about his new friends. Besides, that "dirtbag" of a roommate may turn out to be his best man some day!

You can also help your son as he struggles with his values by encouraging him to find other people on campus who share some of his beliefs. For example, your son might want to talk to the campus's **campus ministry**. The campus ministry staff may be another person your son can talk to about moral dilemmas. At the same time, the chaplain may be able to put your son in touch with other groups or individual students who share the same faith. Usually, the campus chaplain's contact information can be found in the campus directory.

What to expect of your ~~baby~~ young adult in this situation:

* He will talk to you about his values and moral dilemmas.

- He will look for ways to meet people who share some of his values by contacting the chaplain or student organizations that relate to his beliefs.
- He will keep an eye out for lectures and other campus events and activities that address this topic.

Money Issues

My son worked hard at his summer job and saved for his book purchases and spending money for the semester. He also planned on working part time during the school year but has had trouble finding a job. Problem is, he's already running low on cash, and the first month isn't even over yet! Should we bail him out?

It's kind of like when you'd buy a box of Popsicles at the grocery store, and then noticed that they were already gone after only a day or two. Kids have a hard time rationing such treats; likewise, it's hard for young adults to learn how to budget and not spend everything in the first few weeks of the semester. Chalk up financial responsibility as one more area where your son may be testing and experiencing his boundaries and limits while at college.

Your first step is to help him determine where his money is going right now. Did books and supplies cost far more than he budgeted? Is he passing up the less appealing (but paid-for) dining hall food in favor of pizza delivery every night? Did he and his roommate decide to chip in with their suitemates for a new gaming console? Try to help your son get a handle on why most of his money's already spent.

Then, encourage your son to do some further digging for a job on or near campus. He can check with the **financial aid office**, which typically keeps a list of work-study positions available. The restaurants and shops on and around a college campus are often in need of help as well. You may have to help your son manage his job expectations, though. With so many young people around, jobs on or near campus don't have to pay great wages. So, your son may have to start off in a relatively low paying job. That's OK though; as our parents would say to us, "it builds character."

If your son isn't able to find a job, or if the pay isn't enough to cover his needs, then you'll need to consider sending some cash his way so he can make it through the semester. But, you and your son should try to closely track his spending during the remainder of the semester. This will help both of you better prepare for expenses in the future.

What to expect of your ~~baby~~ *young adult in this situation:*

- He will give you an accounting of where his money has gone to this point.
- He will closely track his expenses for the remainder of the semester.
- He will look for a job that meets at least some of his expenses by visiting the financial aid office and local businesses.
- He will report back to you about his job search.

Adjusting To Cultural Differences

My son's roommate is from another country. His background is very different from my son's, and there is even a language barrier between them. I had such hopes for my son to develop a close relationship with his roommate, but I'm not sure this will be possible for them.

In addition to social and academic adjustments, first-year students often also experience cultural adjustments in college. For many young adults, college is the first time that they have been around people who are different from them, in many different ways. Your son's experience is a perfect example of this type of transition.

There may be some cultural differences that your son may notice with his roommate. They may have different styles of communicating, different time habits (for instance, the time of day that it is customary to eat dinner), and different interests. That said, differences of these sorts are common among all roommates, and they require that both people are accommodating and open to change. Being accepting and welcoming of differences is one way to embrace cultural adjustments in college.

Remember when your son started a new grade in school when he was younger? Sometimes it may have been hard to predict who would be his closest buddies that year just based on initial impressions. This may be the same case for your son and his roommate. On the surface, they may not seem to have much in common, but who knows? They may end up being the best of friends.

This relationship also creates a wonderful opportunity for both young men to learn about a new culture. It is not uncommon for students who live closer to campus to invite roommates and friends who are far from home to visit during breaks. For example, your son may invite his room-mate to spend Thanksgiving break at your house. And maybe someday, your son will be invited to visit his roommate in his home country as well.

As you can imagine, it can be a real challenge attending college in a country where you don't speak the language. It will likely take some time for your son's roommate to build up some fluency in his new language, but it will happen. Being immersed in a country with a different language is often the best way for people to become more adept in that language. The lan-guage barrier will likely become less pronounced as the semester goes on.

There is no mention that your son is having a difficult time with his roommate at this point. If he does find that issues are arising, he should consider talking to his RA. The RA can help mediate any difficulties, and support them as they develop (or revise) their roommate contract, or rules of the room. If your son hasn't mentioned that he is having problems, then he is likely rising to the occasion and making this cultural adjustment suc-cessfully. You should be proud of him.

If your son would like to learn more about relating to people who are culturally different from him, he may want to visit the **diversity and inclusion office** on campus. These departments often offer education programming related to diversity issues. Some programs may be of inter-est to your son, who may be experiencing diversity in a new way now.

What to expect of your ~~baby~~ young adult in this situation:

* He will be open and accommodating in regard to the cultural dif-ferences with his roommate.
* He will consider extending invitations to spend time with his roommate, either on campus or at home (or both).

27

* He will be patient with his roommate as he develops his speaking fluency.
* If issues arise with his roommate, he will enlist the help of the RA as needed.
* If he would like to learn more about diversity issues, he will investigate the offerings of the campus diversity and inclusion office.

Step-By-Step . . .

Resident Assistants: Helping Your ~~Baby~~ Young Adult with Separation Anxiety

RAs, or resident assistants, are students, usually undergraduates, who have taken on a leadership role in a residence hall. RAs are typically hired by the **residence hall directors** (professional residential staff members who manage the residence halls) based on their interpersonal and leadership skills, their knowledge of the university and strategies for student success, and their eagerness to help other students.

RAs do lots of things, but on the most basic level, they are the best <u>first</u> resource for your son or daughter. The RA, or "live-in nanny," is your young adult's peer contact person. Each RA is assigned to a group of students in the residence hall (typically assigned according to floor or suite). RAs try to make a personal connection with each resident; they also coordinate group activities for their residents in order to create a sense of community for the floor or suite. Encourage your young adult to go to as many of these RA-sponsored events as possible.

As mentioned throughout this chapter, the RA is a go-to person for all sorts of situations, including:

* Roommate conflicts
* Homesickness
* Information on campus activities, events, groups, clubs and organizations
* Questions on getting around campus and finding necessary resources

If the RA doesn't have the answer to your young adult's question, they have the responsibility and the wealth of resources to investigate further.

STEP-BY-STEP . . .
STUDENT INVOLVEMENT OFFICES: YOUR ~~BABY~~ YOUNG ADULT'S LIFE BEYOND THE CRIB

Universities view student involvement outside the classroom as very important to the growth and satisfaction of students. Research shows that students who participate in campus activities are more satisfied with their college experiences than those who are not (Light, 2001). Because of the value placed on getting students involved, most universities have entire departments focused on student activities and organizations. These departments are typically named, "Office of Student Involvement," "Student Activities," "Student Organization Office," or "Department of Student Life and Recreation." Whatever the name at your young adult's university, this office is the home base for student activities, clubs and organizations. The student involvement office may also supervise Greek life organizations (fraternities and sororities), intramural sports, and community service organizations.

So how to get your young adult out of the crib to utilize the student involvement office and get involved in an organization or club? There are several ways to go about getting linked up with a group. At the beginning of each academic year, many college student involvement offices hold organization fairs. At these events, each activity, club and organization on campus sets up a table or booth, and is on hand to answer questions and recruit new members. Your young adult can shop around at the organization fair to see which groups are a good fit for his or her interests.

Your young adult can also simply stop into the student involvement office, which is usually located in the student union building or student center of the campus. In addition, student involvement offices often list all of their clubs and organizations on their campus website, along with the contact people for each group. They may even be able to follow clubs on social media. Because many student organizations have open enrollment, and are frequently looking for new members, a student can contact the leader or attend a meeting, and join the group.

If you're concerned that your young adult has been spending too much time in the crib, suggest they toddle over to the student involvement office. If they feel uncomfortable doing that alone, maybe they can use the buddy system like they did at summer camp.

CHAPTER 3

October

● ● ●

October 15

Dear M and D,

I AM SO SCREWED! I can't believe it's already mid-semester! My exams aren't going so hot. In fact, I think I failed the math and history exams I took yesterday. My midterm literature paper pretty much sucked, too. How'd I go from being in the top 10 of my senior class to failing out of college in my first semester? It's just that I'm not even sure how I ended up so far behind. I feel like I put in lots of time studying. I even pulled a bunch of all-nighters to cram as much as I could before the math exam, but it didn't get me anywhere. Maybe I'm just not cut out for being a college student.

Andrew

Growing Pains: What May Be Giving Your ~~Baby~~ Young Adult Colic This Month

* Taking midterm exams and receiving midterm grades
* Handling college expenses and money issues
* Questioning: "Do I fit in here?" "Can I make it?"
* Moving out of honeymoon period: life doesn't seem as perfect as it did last month

- Receiving poor grades for the first time ever
- Experiencing continued homesickness
- Falling behind and procrastinating
- Facing roommate problems
- Finding a group of peers to connect with

Procrastination

My daughter has always been a procrastinator when it comes to her school work. In high school, she could fly by the seat of her pants and still manage to get top grades. It seems like her procrastinating habit is catching up with her now, though. I just got an email where she listed all the things she has to finish by Friday. There's no way she'll be able to get them all done. I can tell she's stressed out and feeling in over her head with all of this work. How can I help her?

Your daughter needs help realizing that what worked in high school doesn't necessarily work in college. Many students think that they can continue with the academic habits that earned them high grades in the past, and often experience a rude awakening when they find that college is much more challenging than high school was. Success rates in college are strongly tied to students' time management skills, and your daughter needs some help developing those. Procrastination is a tough habit to break, but it's crucial that she does so if she wants to succeed in college.

The first way that you can support your daughter is by helping her figure out why she's procrastinating. People typically procrastinate for a couple of different reasons: because the task at hand is unpleasant to do or because the task is difficult. Talk to your daughter about what projects or tasks she is procrastinating, and prompt her to examine whether she hates the task ("the reading for history is just soooo boring, Mom!") or feels overwhelmed by it ("I don't even know where to start with this business plan project").

For assignments that are tedious, boring or otherwise unpleasant, talk to your daughter about getting them completed as soon as they are assigned, to get them "out of the way." While you are not there to reward your daughter for her positive behaviors, encourage her to reward herself when she completes her work. For example, if she really likes to watch shows on Netflix, she could make that a reward for finishing reading a chapter of history. Delaying rewards until after work is done may help her with those assignments that she finds unappealing.

For projects that seem difficult and overwhelming, encourage your daughter to list the smaller, more manageable components that make up the project as a whole. For example, for a research paper, she may need to: do research; read the research; develop an outline; meet with her teacher to discuss her plans; write specific sections of the paper; develop a draft; take the draft to the writing center; and polish the paper before handing it in. If she can look at the smaller pieces of the project, she may feel less overwhelmed by it. And, the good news is that there are university services available to help with each step of the process. You can encourage your daughter to get help with research from the **reference librarian**, to visit her professor regularly during **office hours**, and to consult or make an appointment with the **writing center** for help with all aspects of the writing process.

Most of us procrastinate in one area or another of our lives. We usually have some sort of replacement activity that we engage in rather than completing the task that needs doing. Try to help your daughter determine what she is using for her replacement activities instead of doing her course work. Is she texting her boyfriend, watching movie marathons, playing games on her phone? Some of us can be quite industrious while procrastinating; maybe your daughter's replacement activity is something that makes her feel productive, like making sure her room is spotless or helping her roommate with her paper, instead of worrying about her own work. If you can help her identify her procrastination replacement activities, she may be able to monitor these behaviors more closely, and hopefully work to minimize them.

In addition to helping your daughter focus on the tasks she is procrastinating, you should also encourage her to look at her other time management behaviors and habits. College students typically can't keep all of their commitments straight in their heads the way that they may have been able to do in high school. Your daughter should get in the habit of using a calendar or planner to keep track of all of her work. If she doesn't have a calendar, you could send her one or suggest an effective online tool. She will be less likely to forget assignments, and she can also write down the smaller milestones of large projects, so that she won't have all the work still to complete when the due date rolls around. In high school, teachers would typically help students with managing large assignments, but in college, that same responsibility is placed on the student.

You can also talk to your daughter about her daily routines. Probe her with questions about when and where she's getting her studying done. Successful college students typically have set times in their schedules which they commit to coursework. Just as babies are said to thrive on routines, college students thrive on schedules. But instead of you deciding when your baby girl should nap, wake up, eat and play, these decisions are now up to her.

If your daughter can set up a schedule and routine that works well for her, she's likely to become more productive. For example, if she blocks out time in her daily calendar for reading history each week, she will be more likely to complete it. Encourage your daughter to find a regular place outside of her dorm room to study. The residence halls are often full of welcome distractions for students, and are less effective for coursework. Just like naps taken in a crib are usually more restful than those taken in a car seat, the library, academic support center and study lounge are the most efficient places to study.

If you have the sense that your daughter needs some help getting on track with her time management skills, encourage her to talk to her **first-year experience** professor. The first-year experience course often focuses on time management and effective study habits, and the professor for the class may be able to give your daughter some individualized support with this. Another excellent resource for assistance with time management skills is a **learning specialist**. Most universities have an academic support services department or office, with learning specialists who help students look closely at their strategies and habits. A learning specialist can sit down with your daughter and help her develop effective strategies and consistent routines for getting her work done.

What to expect of your ~~baby~~ young adult in this situation:

* She'll take some time to think about what tasks she is procrastinating, and why she is procrastinating these tasks.
* She'll identify her procrastination replacement activities, and work to minimize them.
* She'll develop a routine for her days and will use a calendar to track her reading assignments, papers, quizzes, projects and exams.
* If she's having trouble with any of her projects or assignments, she will seek help from her professor and other campus resources.
* If she's having difficulty developing routines and using her time effectively, she will talk to her First-Year Experience professor or a learning specialist about time management strategies.

FIRST FAILING GRADES EVER

My son has never gotten less than an A during his entire school career. He is in a very challenging pre-med program, and is really nervous about his grades. He has gotten some graded assignments back already, and most of them have been in the B or C range; he has even received F grades on a few quizzes. What is he doing wrong?

Like many first year students, your son hasn't fully made the transition to college-level work yet. Coursework in college requires a different set of skills and a different level of commitment than typical high school level classes.

The first suggestion you can give your son is to track the amount of time he is spending on his studies. First year college students are often surprised to learn that professors expect them to be spending two or three hours of time outside class for every hour they spend in the classroom (Hazard and Nadeau, 2012). So, for students who are taking five classes that meet three hours per week, they should be expecting thirty to forty-five hours of work outside the classroom each week (Hazard and Nadeau, 2012). This time outside of class should be spent reading, studying, doing homework assignments, and preparing for the next class meeting. If your son is spending far less than thirty to forty-five hours per week on his coursework, that is a problem. For certain programs of study, including pre-med, engineering, and finance, the higher end of this time estimate is probably more realistic.

You can also encourage your son to look at what types of study strategies he is using. The difference between high school work and college work is like the difference between crawling and walking. In high school, teachers often provide far more guidance and direction than college professors do. So, college students need to develop the skill of determining what information is important for each course; they also need to develop strategies for processing, understanding and applying the information effectively for each course.

For example, your son may be reading nineteenth century novels for his English class, a highly dense textbook for his organic chemistry class, and *The New York Times* for his political science class. The approaches to these different reading assignments are highly varied, and being able to analyze and apply these varied readings requires flexibility and critical thinking skills. This is vastly different from high school level studying, which is frequently based on memorizing the information provided by the teacher. If your son is relying on his high school strategies, then he is studying inefficiently for his college-level courses.

The **first-year experience** course is designed to help students transition academically to college by teaching them study strategies and skills that will work more effectively in college level courses. Your son would do well to speak with his first-year experience professor about his struggles with his courses; the professor of this course could help him identify ways to change and improve his study habits. The university's **learning specialists**, often located in the academic support services department, also work with students to develop more effective study habits.

Course demands can be discussed during a professor's office hours. In a one on one meeting, your son can get feedback from professors on ways to prepare for quizzes and exams, concepts that are most important for him to understand, and ideas for improving his grades in each course.

Think of the first-year experience instructor as the pediatrician who saw your son for his well visits. Sometimes the pediatrician had to make referrals to other specialists, like to an ear, nose and throat doctor for more specific issues like frequent ear infections. A number of trips to a few different specialists finally determined exactly what was needed, like ear tubes to prevent more infections. Similarly, in college, your son may have to visit his first-year experience instructor, his professor and a learning specialist to discern exactly he needs, like what college level study habits will work best given his learning style and the particular demands of his courses.

What to expect of your baby young adult in this situation:

* He will track the amount of time that he is spending on each course, with the goal of spending three hours per week studying outside of class for each hour in class.
* He will look at his current study strategies, and work with his first-year experience professor and his other course professors to develop study strategies that are more efficient and effective for college-level courses.
* If he needs additional support with learning and applying new study strategies, he will seek out help from a learning specialist.

STRESS ABOUT GRADES

My daughter is really stressed out. After a month of classes, she's worried that she can't do the work expected of a college student. She actually thinks that the admissions office must have made a mistake in accepting her to the college. From what I can tell, her grades are at least average, but she says that's because she is spending every waking moment on her courses. She says that everyone else she knows is doing great with very little effort, and that she has to work harder than everyone else.

The time commitment required for college level studies can be a big adjustment for students like your daughter. College *is* hard work and does take a great deal of time and effort. As discussed previously, professors expect that students are spending around two or three hours working on coursework for every hour spent in the classroom. College is a full-time, forty-plus hour per week job!

So, while your daughter may feel that she's the only one working as hard as she is, that may be because her friends haven't yet committed enough time to their studies. Your daughter may think her friends are doing just fine in their classes, but this is not necessarily the case. Or her friends might not be honest about how much time they are really spending; after all, who wants to admit that they just spent six hours on math problems, and still don't know what the heck it all means? Often, first year college students don't really have a good handle on how they are doing in their classes, and may not be forthcoming with their friends about their grades.

You can commend your daughter for being so dedicated to her education, and suggest that she stop comparing herself to her friends. Remind her that the first semester in college is difficult for most people, even if her friends aren't admitting it. Instead, encourage her to talk to her professors about her academic progress. They will be able to help her assess how well she is doing and may be able to offer suggestions for becoming a more efficient learner.

That said, it sounds like your daughter is experiencing an uncomfortable amount of stress at this point. She may need to rethink the way she is spending her time. Encourage your daughter to track the time she spends on school work for a week or so. If she is spending around thirty to forty-five hours per week on her classes, then she is probably on target for the required work assigned. And believe it or not, if your daughter is taking thirty to forty-five hours per week to complete her schoolwork, then she still has plenty of time for rest and relaxation. Hazard and Nadeau (2009) encourage first-year college students to follow the 8-8-8 formula, which stresses balance by equally dividing the 24 hour day into three components: coursework, sleep and leisure.

Think back to when your daughter was a newborn. When you brought her home from the hospital, it may have been difficult to find a balanced schedule for her at first. Babies need lots of sleep, mental and physical stimulation, and nurturing. Too much or too little of any of these leads to a cranky baby. Same goes with college students. They need adequate sleep, enough time for their classes and time to have some fun. If a student is spending 8 hours per day in classes and on coursework, and 8 hours per day sleeping, then that leaves 8 hours per day for leisure. If your daughter can strike this balance, and give herself permission to relax, then her stress level should decrease as well.

If your daughter hasn't already found an on-campus activity that she enjoys participating in during her free time, she may want to look for one. Often just having fun, in and of itself, will relieve some stress. If there's something that she liked to do in high school, chances are that there is an organization on campus with other students who share this interest. Your daughter can talk to her resident assistant about her interests, and ask the RA for suggestions on what groups or activities would be a good fit for her.

Your daughter may find that she is spending far more time than thirty to forty-five hours per week on her coursework, and still feels like she is barely hanging on; if this is the case, she needs to take a closer look at her study strategies. As mentioned previously in this chapter, high school work often provides students with a different set of skills than what is needed to succeed in college. If your daughter is not feeling like her hard work is really paying off in the way of good grades, then she may want to look more closely at her study skills.

For example, maybe your daughter always did really well on her high school tests by preparing index cards with each idea or fact she needed to learn, or commit to memory. She would then flip through all the index cards until she knew them all by heart. This time-consuming task served her well in high school, but because college tests are less about memorization and more about analysis and critical thinking, this strategy may not produce the same results. So, no matter how many index cards she makes, and no matter how many time she flips through them, she will not be processing the information in a way that will help her do well on a college test. She needs a new approach to studying, where the time and effort she puts in pays off with the grade she wants. Your daughter's First-Year Experience professor and the learning specialist at the university's academic services office can help her assess and improve her study skills. This may allow her to get her coursework completed more effectively and efficiently.

If your daughter finds that the academic stress continues to interfere with her life and her ability to enjoy herself, then she may benefit from the support of talking with someone in the university's **counseling services** office. The professionals who work in university counseling can help her to identify stressors and to develop the tools to relieve this stress.

What to expect of your ~~baby~~ young adult in this situation:

* She will meet with her professors to assess her academic progress.
* She will track the amount of time she is studying for a week to see how much time she is spending on her academics.
* She will allow herself time to relax and find activities that she enjoys.
* If she is spending more than forty-five hours per week on her courses, she will discuss her present study strategies with her First-Year Experience professor or the university's learning specialist.
* If she feels that her stress is interfering with her life and her ability to enjoy herself, then she will visit the university's counseling services office.

Honeymoon's Over

My son seemed to be having the time of his life for the first few weeks of school. Now, when he texts or calls me, he sounds really negative. He says he hates his classes and he seems to not be hanging out with the same group of guys that he first met on move-in day. What's the matter with him?

It sounds like the college honeymoon is over and reality may be setting in for your son. The first few weeks of college are so novel and exciting; then, the exhilaration wears off, and first-year students can sometimes tumble back down to earth. It's like when your son got a new toy for his birthday. He may have loved it and played with it during every waking moment – for the first few days or weeks. Then, after a while, he lost interest, and you later found it collecting dust at the bottom of the toy box. Novelties wear off.

The first thing that you as a parent can do to help is to find out more about what is turning off your son about college. Do a little probing to find out where the negativity is coming from. Are his classes very difficult or less stimulating than he expected? Has he found that the group of friends he originally formed has different interests than he does? Is the college atmosphere different from those early fall days? Is the dining hall food just too awful for words? When you have a better idea of where his emotions are coming from, you can better offer support to him. And talking with you may help him understand his own feelings as well.

You can also offer your son praise and encouragement for his progress to date. Remind him that going to college and living away from home is hard work and a huge adjustment. You can also point out to him the rewards that come at the end of the semester, including earning good grades for good work, and being able to come home for the break, where he can sleep as much as he wants and hang out with all his old buddies.

Encourage your son to set concrete social and academic goals to help him get through the rest of the semester. For example, if he really isn't hitting it off with the group of guys that he met originally, then his goal may be to join a club so that he can meet people that share his interests. You can talk to him about what he liked to do in high school and suggest that he look for a comparable organization on his campus. For example, if he really liked working on his high school yearbook, he may want to look into joining the college yearbook group.

If your son is feeling very negative about his academics, he could set goals related to improving his grades. He could plan to visit his professors' **office hours**, approach some classmates about forming a study group, or find a tutor who can help him with that math course. Once he's set these social and academic goals, you can offer support by periodically asking about his progress and by helping him track his successes.

You can also suggest that your son discuss his experiences with his **RA**. He will likely find that he is not alone in feeling that the honeymoon is over. The RA likely experienced it himself at some point in his own first year. The RA may also be able to offer your son some other suggestions for meeting people and for how to approach his classes.

What to expect of your ~~baby~~ young adult in this situation:

* He will do some self-examination to identify the sources of his negative feelings about college.
* He will set goals for the rest of the semester, and utilize the campus resources that will help him reach these goals.
* He will agree to periodic check-ins with you to see if the situation has improved.
* He will discuss his negative feelings and experiences with his RA.

ROOMMATE RELATIONSHIPS

In the first few weeks of school, my daughter and her roommate were inseparable. They met at orientation in June, and hit it off great from the start. From the time they moved in, they ate together, worked out together, studied together and went out on weekends together. Now, from some of the comments my daughter has made to me over the phone, it sounds like her roommate is ditching her for some other young women who live down the hall. My daughter is upset and confused that her roommate doesn't seem to want to be her best friend anymore.

Living with someone who was a stranger only a few weeks ago can be difficult. It may take a while until roommates really feel like they know one another. Once a sense of familiarity develops after a month or so, roommate relationships can change. On top of that, each first year student is in the process of self-discovery, and of trying to reinvent themselves; they are making the transformation from high school kid to a young adult college student. As individuals like your daughter and her roommate each undergo this process, they may find that they have less in common than they originally thought. This is common in any type of friendship (remember how your daughter may have lost touch with her pre-school playmates once she went to kindergarten?), and is sometimes accelerated by the intensity of being with a roommate on a constant basis.

You can help your daughter to realize that roommates don't always have to be best friends. Sometimes spending every waking moment with someone can get tiresome; while your daughter may not have felt that way, hopefully you can help her understand that people often need a break from one another.

If your daughter can try to adjust her expectations of this relationship, she will not feel so let down by the roommate. Encourage her to reach out to the roommate to see if they can strike a better balance. Instead of trying to do everything together, perhaps they can agree on one or two activities that they would like to do together. Maybe the two of them can plan on eating breakfast together if they both have the same early class. Or, they can plan to spend Sunday afternoons studying in the library together. The roommate may be happy to spend some time with your daughter, but may not have known how to set comfortable limits with her.

Like your daughter's roommate, your daughter also needs to find her own set of friends. She should make a concerted effort to get involved with alternative activities on her own, rather than solely relying on her roommate to be her friend. As mentioned before, a tried and true strategy is to revisit the activities she's enjoyed in the past, and find a group on campus that is involved in such activities. While one of the purposes of college is to explore new experiences, people, and interests, it's still important to continue with the activities that make your daughter who she is. For example, if you camped as a family, your daughter may want to join the university's outdoor activity club. By taking the initiative to find her own friends, your daughter will build confidence and feel less dependent on her roommate.

Your daughter's **RA** can also support your daughter with this issue. The RA can mediate any conflicts that may arise between your daughter and her roommate, and can suggest organizations or clubs that would be a good fit for her interests. In addition, the RA can help by introducing your daughter to other students who live in the same residence hall. Who knows? Your daughter's new best friend might be just one floor down!

What to expect of your ~~baby~~ young adult in this situation:

- She will make an effort to talk to her roommate and find ways that they can spend some time together, rather than all of their time together.
- She will look for an activity or club that would provide her with the opportunity to make friends who share her interests.
- She will talk to her RA about the changes in her relationship with her roommate.

Get A Job?

My daughter has been offered a job working at the front desk of her residence hall. She seems quite concerned about money and being able to pay for all of her incidental expenses, but I'm concerned that she won't be concentrating enough on her studies. I wish she'd just cut back on her spending and not worry about holding down a job during her first semester.

Remember when your daughter asked you if she could start babysitting to earn money to go to the mall? You were worried if she was ready to handle that kind of job, but she managed just fine. Usually, when somebody expresses a desire to take on more responsibility, it's an indication that they may be ready for it.

There are expenses that go along with living at college – toiletries, birthday presents, pizza – that your daughter is probably no longer relying on you to help with. That's a good thing! A job may help her feel more independent and allow her the experience of managing her own money, as long as the work doesn't interfere with her academic success.

Campus jobs are typically designed for students' busy schedules. Work study jobs usually allow some time for homework, and most universities limit the number of hours per week that students can work. Some studies have shown that working part-time on campus does not negatively impact a student's academic performance in college, as long as the number of hours is limited. These studies show that students working 10 to 20 hours per week continue to perform well academically (Van de Water, 1996; Hood, Craig and Ferguson, 1992). In fact, some studies show that students who work part-time on their college campuses tend to have higher GPAs than those who do not work part-time (Perozzi, Rainey and Wahlquist, 2003).

There are benefits, beyond the financial, to working a part-time work study job. Some students find that when they are at their jobs, they actually get more academic work done, because there are fewer distractions than they would encounter in their dorm rooms. Today's college students are good at multitasking, and the idea of getting paid for a work-study job while getting homework done at the same time can be very appealing! And because college students thrive on structure and schedules, having a job commitment to consider may also help your daughter build a schedule that allows for all of her obligations, rather than having unstructured days that are only broken up by having to get to class. As the saying goes, "If you want something done, ask a busy person."

Perozzi, Rainey and Wahlquist (2003) also note studies indicating that on-campus part-time jobs help students feel more connected to their college communities, and provide additional opportunities to meet other students, faculty and staff. By working at the front desk of her residence hall, your daughter will likely get to know the residence hall's RAs, the residence hall director, and many of the other students who live there.

In helping your daughter make this decision, suggest that she find out some additional information about the job. You could encourage her to ask the following questions: How many hours a week will I be expected to work? Can I do homework during quiet times on the job? If I have an exam or other academic commitment, are there provisions for changing hours? If she is comfortable with the answers to these questions, then this job could work out well for her.

If your daughter does decide to take the job, encourage her to monitor her grades very closely for the remainder of the semester, and to commit to leaving the job if she cannot continue to do well in her courses.

What to expect of your ~~baby~~ young adult in this situation:

* She will find out more about the job before deciding to take it.
* If she does take the job, she will not work more than 20 hours per week, and she will monitor her grades closely, and leave the job if her coursework is suffering.

Step-By-Step . . .
Academic Support Services: Helping Your ~~Baby~~ Young Adult Clean Up Their Academic Messes

Universities today recognize the importance of providing academic support beyond what is offered in the classroom. At about 70% of universities, there are departments that provide a variety of services to students who want to improve their academic skills. Some are as large as an entire campus building while others are as small as a table in the library. Each university calls its department by a different name; some examples of department names include: Academic Excellence Center, Tutoring Center, Learning Center, Academic Support Center or University Learning Commons. Whatever the name and wherever the location, strongly encourage your young adult to seek out the academic support services at their institution and use them. If your son or daughter is not sure how to find out more about academic support services, they can talk to their RA or to their First-Year Experience professor.

Many people associate tutoring and learning support with the remedial services available to high school and middle school students whose grades are not up to par. University academic services are quite different, and are provided to all students, usually free of charge, no matter what their ability or skill level. In a college's academic support services center, one can expect to see students of all skill levels working on all types of tasks and projects. It may surprise your son or daughter to learn that the first tutoring center was founded at Harvard University. It would not be unusual for a professor to refer students to tutoring, as faculty typically view such visits to academic support centers quite positively.

While these centers vary from university to university, most academic support centers offer a core of services to students, for individuals and for groups of students. Often, the center will have a learning specialist on staff; these staff members work with students on their academic and study skills, and can help first year students make the transition to the demands of college-level courses. **Learning specialists** provide students support with managing their time, getting organized, taking tests and notes, listening to lectures, and developing effective study habits. If the university doesn't have a learning specialist, workshops may be offered to deliver the same information. If your daughter or son is having difficulty in any of these areas, meeting with a learning specialist or attending a workshop are great solutions.

Because many college courses require a great deal of reading, academic support centers may provide specialized support in developing reading skills. Often, first year students stagger under the sheer weight of the reading that they are expected to complete, and have a great deal of difficulty reading for both quantity and quality. So, if your young adult is telling you about how they are feeling overwhelmed by the reading, encourage them to make an appointment with the university's reading specialist or attend a workshop focused on reading strategies.

Academic support centers almost always provide tutoring for classes that tend to be challenging to students. A tutor can be a professional staff person or another student, with experience in the course content and training in tutoring strategies. Usually tutoring is most effective when a student makes tutoring part of their academic routine; that is, the student needs to meet with a tutor regularly in order to see the benefits reflected in their course grade.

Similar to tutoring services, most universities offer writing center services as well. Professors often have different expectations of writing projects than teachers in high school, and tutors in the writing center can help your young adult build their writing skills. Writing tutors work with students to identify their own strengths and challenges with their writing assignments and to help them develop writing strategies that work well in college.

Studies have shown that students who do use academic support services, particularly in their first year, have higher grades and higher rates of graduation than students who don't (Cuseo, 2003). You can help your son or daughter to achieve their academic goals by encouraging them to identify their own academic challenges; whatever their particular academic challenge may be, the university's academic support center can likely provide them with the support they need.

STEP-BY-STEP . . .
PROFESSORS' OFFICE HOURS: TEACHING YOUR ~~BABY~~ YOUNG ADULT HOW TO TALK TO FACULTY WITHOUT WETTING THEIR PANTS

At most universities, professors are required to have weekly scheduled office hours, which are set times that they are available in their offices to meet individually with students from their classes. Professors typically post these scheduled hours on their syllabi, on their office doors and/or on the course web pages.

The idea of speaking individually to a professor may seem intimidating, but strongly encourage your young adult to do so. Sometimes it's difficult for students to engage with faculty members in the classroom; often, the professor may leave the room right after class ends, or is flooded with students asking individual questions. A better time to converse with faculty members is during the times that they have set aside for this purpose: office hours.

A visit to a professor's office hours can be useful in many ways. If your young adult:

- is in a very large class, the professor can meet with students individually, and start associating names with faces.
- is having difficulty with the content of the course, the professor can better tailor an explanation of the content to a student's individual learning style.
- is preparing for an exam or presentation, the professor can answer specific questions.

- is writing a paper, the professor can read the outline or rough draft to help ensure students are on the right track.
- is especially interested in a topic discussed in class, the professor can help engage your young adult's intellectual curiosity by discussing it further and perhaps suggesting additional resources.
- did poorly on a paper, exam or other assignment, the professor can explain how to improve in the future.

Your son or daughter may be hesitant at first to visit a professor's office hours, but you can support them with this by assuring them that faculty LOVE when students come to their office hours. Often faculty are in their offices, with no students taking advantage of this time. When a student does come to office hours, the faculty member is typically pleased to see them and give them all the time they need.

Some additional information to pass along to your young adult about office hours:

- If possible, let the faculty member know in advance that they are planning to visit during office hours on a particular day.
- Come to office hours with specific questions, concerns or assignments to discuss. This could be as simple as, "I was wondering how I am doing in your course, and what I can do to improve," or "I am struggling with the concept of supply-side economics from last week's class, and would appreciate it if you could please help me clarify this idea a bit more."
- Bring all course materials to office hours, including textbook, notebook, and previous assignments, exams and papers.
- If the faculty member's office hours conflict with their schedule, contact the professor to schedule an alternate time to meet instead.

In addition to full professors, many colleges have other staff members teaching courses, including adjunct faculty and teaching assistants (TAs). Adjuncts are part time faculty members who teach one or more courses at a university each semester. Because they do not work at the university on a full-time basis, their office hours are not always as frequent or accessible as other faculty members' hours. If your young adult has an adjunct faculty member, they may have to make an extra effort to arrange a meeting that fits the adjunct's tight schedule.

A TA assists a full faculty member with a course, and has some grading, teaching and meeting duties. TAs are often graduate students, and they work as teaching assistants in their fields of study. Some classes that are quite large tend to have TAs assigned to them, so that students can get individualized attention beyond what the faculty member can provide. Like professors, TAs often have scheduled office hours, and can be very helpful in assisting students with the same concerns that professors do. Encourage your young adult to refer to the course syllabi for guidance on whether they should be meeting with their TA or with the professor (or both).

CHAPTER 4

November

● ● ●

November 10

Dear Mom,

I totally screwed up. Now I don't know what to do. I had a quiz in chemistry yesterday and I slept right through it. I've had a horrible cold, so I took some medicine for my cough. I was up practically all night studying and my room-mate offered me a beer. She and her friends ALWAYS have a few beers before they go to bed. I didn't really want one 'cause I felt like crap, but everyone was hanging out in my room while I was studying, so I figured, "What's the big deal? I'll just have one." I know you've always told me not to mix alcohol with medicine, but I didn't think one would hurt. That's why I slept through the alarm. I didn't even hear it!

What should I do? I have no clue how much getting a zero on that quiz is going to affect my grade. I feel like such an idiot. I am so embarrassed. Not to mention, I totally hate chemistry to begin with. Please don't tell Dad. I liked science in high school, but now I hate it. I really don't want to be pre-med anymore. The only class I like is anthropology. I have to register for classes next week. I don't want to take organic chemistry next semester.

If I suck at regular chemistry, what will that be like? What do I do? I don't even want to come back here after Thanksgiving............

Love,
Kendra

Growing Pains: What May Be Causing Your ~~Baby's~~ Young Adult's Meltdowns This Month

* Doubting choice about major field of study or experiencing anxiety about not having already decided on a major
* Registering for second semester classes
* Encountering the first wave of campus wide illnesses
* Feeling the pressure of exams, papers, assignments or projects due before Thanksgiving
* Recognizing that finals are just around the corner and first-semester is nearly over
* Wondering if this particular college is really the place for them
* Experiencing consequences of some bad decisions
* Mounting academic pressure because of procrastination, difficulty of workload, or lack of ability
* Increasing alcohol consumption as a way to relieve stress
* Feeling tension within the residence halls as students begin to get on each other's nerves with increased academic pressure
* Feeling restless for vacation; your young adult may be excited about going home or afraid to face you due to poor grades

COMMUNICATING WITH PROFESSORS

My daughter was sick and missed a quiz in her class. She is very worried about how this will affect her grade. What should she do?

As was mentioned in the last chapter, professors normally have office hours recorded on their syllabi indicating when they are available to speak one-on-one with students. Your daughter needs to speak directly with the professor to find out what his/her exact policy is regarding missed assignments, quizzes or tests. Some professors have their make-up policies clearly spelled out on their syllabi; for others, the policy might not be as explicit. In either case, your daughter should find out when the office hours are and arrange to speak with the professor. Advise that she send off a polite e-mail (in formal English, NOT in "e-speak"!) to the professor beforehand letting them know that she will be coming in to talk about the missed assignment.

If possible, it's always best to let the professor know in advance that an assignment will be missed, but there are sometimes situations where this is not possible, such as an emergency or illness. Like you did when she was little, tell your daughter that "honesty is always the best policy." When it comes to speaking with professors, particularly seasoned professors, and students' attempts to "snow job" them, they are able to see right through the contrived explanations. Counsel your daughter to first and foremost admit to the mistake and take responsibility for her actions. The professor is more likely to be flexible or make exceptions to steadfast rules, like allowing an opportunity to make up the work, if the student approaches the situation with earnestness. Still, there is always the possibility that the professor will not make exceptions to rules already recorded on the syllabus. Unfortunately, if this is the case, your daughter will have to live with the results of her mistake.

Should you intervene at this point? Absolutely not. This situation is one where your daughter will have to learn from the consequences and handle the situation differently next time.

What to expect of your ~~baby~~ young adult in this situation:

* She will e-mail her professor to let themr know that she will be coming to office hours.
* She will be honest with her professor about the situation and take full responsibility for her actions.
* She will tell the professor that she fully understands why there are strict policies in place, but ask respectfully for a second chance.

❖ If the professor denies the chance to make up the work, your daughter will thank them for the opportunity to discuss the situation (chances are, the professor will remember the maturity with which she handled the circumstances at grading time). If a make-up is granted, your daughter will thank them profusely for the opportunity.

CAMPUS ILLNESSES

My son is really sick. We live too far away for him to come home and go to his regular doctor. What should he do?

Almost all colleges and universities have places on campus located in a **health services department** or **health center** where your son will be able to seek medical attention. Recall earlier in the year when you were filling out the paper work to prepare your son to enter college. Among this documentation were medical forms that you likely had to sign to release your son's records to the university. This is much like what you had to do when your little one was going to kindergarten. You had to let the school know that all of his shots and immunizations were up-to-date and alert school personnel to whether he had any allergies or special dietary restrictions. When you sent this information to the university, it was likely forwarded to the health services department.

Depending on the size of the university, this department is typically staffed with nurses, nurse practitioners, physician assistants, and medical doctors. These departments function in a somewhat similar manner to a local urgent care, walk-in clinic or emergency center. Usually if a student isn't feeling well, they can just go to the department without an appointment and be seen on that same day. Your son should locate the website of this department on his campus to find out the hours of their walk-in services and whether they are free.

Keep in mind that if your son lives on campus, he is in a similar situation to when he was little if he went to a daycare center for his child care. Residence halls and dorm rooms are germ factories. There are tens of hundreds of students living in very close proximity to each other. Instead of having the luxury of going home at the end of the day after such close contact with their playmates and friends, they are living with them. It is very important for college students to be mindful of practicing good health habits, such as covering noses and mouths with tissues while coughing or sneezing, avoiding close contact with sick friends, thorough hand-washing, and staying home from classes when sick in an effort to limit contact with others to keep from infecting them. If students do decide to stay home from class, it is wise for them to go to the **health services department** and get a doctor's note.

What to expect of your ~~baby~~ young adult in this situation:

- He will find out the hours of his health services department and come to an understanding of how this department functions on his campus.
- He will be mindful of practicing the good health habits you taught him when he was a child.
- He will avoid contact with other sick students in the event of a campus wide illness.
- He will stay home from classes to avoid infecting other students when he is sick.
- If he does miss classes due to an illness, he will email professors in advance and obtain a doctor's note from his health services department.

USING ALCOHOL AS A STRESS RELIEF

My daughter is very stressed about her grades because final exams are right around the corner. I have been calling her periodically to check in to see how she is doing. Every time I call, it sounds like there is a party going on in her room (while she is studying!!!). She assures me everything is alright and they are just chillin', having a couple of beers while they are preparing for class. I have never heard her talk so much about alcohol. Is this normal?

On most campuses, alcohol is a big part of the culture. There are certain times of the semester when alcohol consumption tends to increase.

Typically, students use alcohol to celebrate reunions after being apart from each other on breaks. So, at the beginning of each semester, parties crop up everywhere. Students also use alcohol to mark rituals such as the end of mid-terms or finals. Of course weekends are when college campuses are really hopping. You may also hear references to the weekly party scene on campuses. On some campuses, aside from weekends, there are particular weekday nights that are the popular nights to go out. Some students have nicknamed these nights, "Wasted Wednesdays" or "Thirsty Thursdays." It must sound like college students are drinking seven days a week. So, is this normal? That's a very good question. In short, alcohol is embedded in the college culture, and on some campuses, this atmosphere sets up the ability for students to party every night of the week if they chose to.

According to the 2000 College Alcohol Survey (Anderson & Gadaleto), college and university administrators estimate that alcohol is involved with: 30% of drop outs, 36% of academic failures, 60% of violent behaviors, 64% of unsafe sexual practices, and 70% of acquaintance rapes. Moreover, the misuse of alcohol by underage students remains a problem for some in spite of laws, campus policies and college programs. So although this drinking behavior is not "normal," it is the norm on many campuses and can be the impetus for many problems your daughter may face if she gets caught up in this part of the campus culture.

Rather than focusing on whether the amount of drinking is normal, a better question might be, have you talked with your daughter about drinking in college? The Foundation for Advancing Alcohol Responsibility (responsibility.org) recommends that you share your own experiences with drinking, both positive and negative. Communicate your family's beliefs and values relative to alcohol consumption. Above all, clearly relay your expectations about such things as attending classes, drinking and driving, financial responsibility, choices regarding drinking, and study time vs. social time. The rationale behind this is that it is better to have an open line of communication so that your young adult can be well-informed in their decisions about alcohol.

If you have not had the experience of having frank conversations with your children about this issue or are feeling awkward about discussing it with them, The Foundation for Advancing Alcohol Responsibility suggests the following conversation starters:

- How do you decide whether or not to drink at college?
- What would you do if you find yourself at a party with only alcohol to drink?
- What would you do if your roommate only wants to drink and party?
- What would you do if you find a student passed out in the bathroom?
- How would you handle it if you are asked to baby-sit someone who is very drunk?

Remember, you are not alone. Your daughter can speak one-on-one with her **RA** or her **first-year experience** course instructors if she has concerns about how to handle the alcohol culture on campus. Rest assured, universities are well aware that alcohol usage is a concern on college campuses. Alcohol awareness education abounds on the majority of campuses. Your job is to get your daughter to tune in.

Many campuses have wellness programs where health educators deliver wellness education via some type of **wellness center**. Chances are this department first addressed the topic of alcohol at your birthing classes (orientation). During orientation, students were probably told how to get help on campus and how to refuse a drink. Orientation was likely used to start the conversation. Remember though, students are so overwhelmed with information at this point in their college careers. We advise that you may very well have to revisit orientation information with them again.

No matter what you do, the possibility exists that your daughter will take some risks. When you cautioned her to always wear a helmet while riding a bike, you were trying to shield her from danger, yet sometimes you saw her flying down the hill without a helmet. Constant reminders finally got her in the routine of riding safely. So if she does experiment with alcohol and is flying high, you want to bring her back down to earth and enforce the message that she needs to protect herself from the potential dangers of drinking.

What do we know and what do they need to know? Research says that the majority of college students do make responsible decisions about alcohol usage. Still, the availability of alcohol, the absence of parents, and the desire to fit in may lead to potentially risky drinking decisions. Talk to them about how to distinguish between low and high risk drinking. If you feel uncomfortable, refer them to the experts on campus who can stress the following information (from The Foundation for Advancing Alcohol Responsibility):

Low-risk drinking is:

- Thinking about whether you will drink, what you will drink before the party
- Being 21 or older
- Eating a meal before drinking
- Drinking no more than one drink per hour; maximum 1 for women, 2 for men
- Always knowing what you are drinking
- Alternating alcohol-free drinks throughout the evening
- Knowing how you will get home safely before you go out

High-risk drinking is:

- Chugging, drinking games, taking shots (drinking out of a punch bowl, trough, hose, or funnel)
- Drinking to get drunk (intoxicated)
- Driving after drinking or riding with someone under the influence
- Drinking too much too fast
- Going to parties where people drink too much
- Not knowing what is in your glass or leaving it unattended
- Mixing alcohol with medications or illegal substances

What to expect of your ~~baby~~ young adult in this situation:

- She'll have a conversation with you about the amount and frequency of the alcohol that she has been consuming.
- She will remove herself from her room to do her studying if her room seems to be the hub for "chillin." If she does not want her room to continue to be the center of "having a few beers while studying each night," she'll talk to her roommate and RA.
- She will talk to you, a health educator, or attend a campus alcohol program to help her understand the difference between high and low risk drinking.

DECIDING ON A MAJOR FIELD OF STUDY

My son called me the other day feeling so lost. He went off to college intending on majoring in engineering, but now says he hates all of his math and science courses. He is also struggling in them, which surprises me because those were ALWAYS his strongest subjects. He is so confused. Now, he's talking about changing his major and even questioning whether this college is the best place for him. I feel so helpless that I can't fix this for him. He sounded so down. What do I say to him?

We can't stress enough that college is a huge adjustment. Most students are shocked when they find out the amount of work required for success in college courses and could have never anticipated the difference in the level of difficulty between high school and college. A few things might be happening. First, as you said, if these subject areas always came very easily to him, there's a chance that he is not putting in the necessary amount of time that is required to be successful in courses at this level. In other words, if he excelled in these subject areas in high school with little or no effort, and is doing the same now, it is not surprising that in college, little or no effort would not yield the same results. He may just have to accept that he has to step it up to get A's and B's in subjects that once came very easily to him. See if you can find out if this is the case.

If he is putting in the time and effort (three hours for every hour of course work), he may need to seek out tutoring. Assure him that this is very normal. The majority of first-year students need to seek out the help of academic support services as they make the academic transition from high school to college. Right now, it is likely that his self-esteem is suffering a little. If he always thought of himself as a strong math and science student, and his grades aren't reflecting that part of his self-concept, this can bring about disheartening feelings. In addition, if he has always been a strong student in these areas, he probably has never had to ask for help. This is when a little humility is necessary. Let him know we all have to ask for help at one time or another. Share an instance where you have had to admit defeat and ask for support.

Above all, be sure to clearly communicate to him that not having initial success in those courses does not mean he has to panic and change his major; it is very early in his college career. Try to keep him from falling into a "catastrophizing" mode. Aside from you, he may need someone to talk to regarding this confusion about his major.

November is usually the time when students are registering for spring semester courses. He may be nervous about picking out classes when he is having this "crisis" about his major. The good news is when students register, they are often required to meet with an **academic advisor**. Most colleges and universities have an advising system to help students plan their educational career. In addition to course selections, these professionals can help students define or in some cases redefine academic goals. Advising systems vary widely across college campuses. For instance, on some campuses, advisors are faculty members, while others are professionals with advanced degrees in counseling, higher education administration, or student development. The good news is that almost all campuses have an individual that can help your son navigate through this….let's call it a "mini-crisis."

Finally, if through a little soul searching, conversations with you, and meeting with his academic advisor, your son feels like he is done with the sciences, and completely wants to switch gears, you may want to refer him to the career services department on campus. **Career services** departments are designed to help students explore their interests. Many students come to college without having decided on a major and this is normal. Remember when he was little and you helped him explore his interests? Should he sign up for art, music, soccer, or hockey? You helped him dabble. Well, the academic advisor can help him dabble in coursework to explore his interests and career services can administer interest inventories to dig a little deeper, only this time it won't be digging in the sand box, it'll be digging into his passion.

What to expect of your ~~baby~~ young adult in this situation:

* He will self-reflect on the amount of effort he has put into his courses.
* He will consider seeking out tutoring.
* He will meet with his academic advisor to discuss course planning and registration.
* He will go to career services to investigate taking an interest inventory.

STEP-BY-STEP . . .

HEALTH SERVICES: WHEN YOUR PEDIATRICIAN IS ON VACATION

As mentioned, all college and universities have health services on campus to care for your young adult in the absence of their regular doctors. Usually, there is no fee for services offered. Though these departments function much like urgent care facilities, most are also concerned with the overall well-being of students. These departments will not only be there for your young adult when they are sick, they will also work to get them healthy and help them to stay healthy.

Typically, students must be registered for classes to have access to health care. Most universities require accident and sickness insurance. Still, many universities advise students to maintain adequate health insurance to cover unexpected medical expenses. In the event of a medical emergency, health services departments are able to make referrals to hospitals or specialists in the community.

Aside from caring for your young adult when they get sick on campus, this department can assist you if they suffer from a chronic illness. When you fill out your university's health forms, be sure to mention any special health circumstances or dietary restrictions your first-year may have. Finally, a wonderful service that can be found on many health services' websites is a vehicle for students to register with their campus department to receive health alerts. These health alerts will let your young adult know if a flu virus has broken out on campus or if there a concern about an outbreak of strep throat. Awareness is the key to prevention!

STEP-BY-STEP . . .
WELLNESS CENTER: PREVENTING YOUR ~~BABY~~ YOUNG ADULT FROM GETTING A DIAPER RASH

Most colleges and universities have programs and services to promote student wellness. These programs may be delivered out of a stand-alone department such as a **wellness center** or may be affiliated with another campus department such as health services or athletics. The goal of these departments is to assist students in making healthy choices to develop a healthy lifestyle that includes eating well, getting enough sleep, exercising, and reducing stress in order to promote success inside and outside of the classroom (DiPrete). Programs delivered out of a department like this might include workshops with topics ranging from stress management to healthy sexual behavior. The point is, these departments typically take a wide view of what it means to be healthy beyond exercising regularly and eating right.

Wellness in this sense is more of a way of life or a philosophy to be followed. There are several facets of life students should examine if they feel they are not doing well. In these departments, there is likely a person your young adult could go talk to if they have concerns about a particular aspect of their wellness. Chances are this person will guide them into thinking about their physical, emotional, social, intellectual, and even their spiritual lives. So yes, a person should be exercising regularly, but in terms of emotional health, your young adult may think about their friendships and ask themselves if the friends they have chosen at college are indeed positive influences on their lives. Healthy relationships, for example, are considered a part of overall wellness.

How about sleep? Should your baby be napping at this point in their lives? If they are napping, it is likely they are sleep deprived; it is well documented that the college population is one of the most sleep deprived groups around. The human adult needs about eight hours of sleep a night. If your babies need naps, it is likely because they are up too late studying . . . or doing other things (you fill in the blank). Getting up for early classes is a challenge if you go to bed when the sun is coming up. Lack of sleep has serious consequences, such as crankiness (oh, you remember how your baby used to be without enough sleep) or even worse, memory impairment, lack of focus and concentration. If your young adult is sleep deprived, a professional in the wellness center can help them figure out why. Is it stress? Use of alcohol? Caffeine? If they are sleep deprived, their lives are out of balance. A wellness professional can help them restore this balance.

Living a balanced life such as eating right, getting enough sleep, and cultivating healthy relationships is the key to wellness. So no, you are not there to check if your baby is wet. This time, you can't prevent the diaper rash, but a health educator in the wellness center may be able to help them to think about the choices they are making that could lead to more serious discomfort.

Step-By-Step . . .
Academic Advising: Cloth or Disposable? Making Tough Decisions

Colleges and universities have **advising services** or **advising centers** to help students navigate through the myriad of academic issues they will face during their four years of college. From application to graduation, advisors collaborate with students to assist them in identifying their educational goals. This activity of advising engages the student's decision-making process. The main purpose of academic advising, whether the advisor is a faculty member or professional staff member, is to guide the students to make deliberative decisions about their academic, social, and career choices. A student may have to make a decision as simple as, "What courses should I take this semester? or as complicated as, "If I study abroad my junior year, how will this affect my progress toward completing my degree in four years?"

Although advisors explain policies of the university and specific requirements of individual programs of study, good advising promotes student success by providing critical information, addressing a wide variety of problems, making appropriate referrals, and hopefully fostering student responsibility and an appreciation for lifelong learning. So, a student asking the question of "what courses should I take this semester?" sounds simple, right? Well, a good advisor will know how to ask questions to find out if the answer is simple; it may not be. Students may have to carefully think through their decisions. Consider a first year student who has always hated history, but taking a history course is a requirement for the degree. Like we want students to do, the student takes responsibility at the advising session and announces that they have always hated history, so they will take it first semester to get that dreaded course out of the way.

The first year is a tough transition. The goal at most colleges and universities is to help students maximize the potential for success during the first year. A seasoned advisor knows this and may get the student to try to think about taking courses they know they will enjoy during the first year as opposed to the dreaded ones, to insure that smooth transition and to help the student build confidence. So, although the advisor will make recommendations to your young adult, the ultimate decision rests with them. Unlike YOUR choice of cloth or disposable, this time, your young adult's decisions are all their own. They will have to deliberatively go through the implications of their choices. Is cloth really better for the environment? What about the soap suds? The good news is the advisor will help your baby find a detergent that's phosphate free if cloth is the way they want to go!

CHAPTER 5

December

● ● ●

December 3

Dear Mom and Dad,

I can't believe my first semester is almost over! I know I still have a ton of school stuff to do, but it should be fine, right? I mean, they give us almost two weeks off, and I just have five exams that whole time.

It's gotten a lot more fun around here, too. I went with Kevin and Mike to a "Holidays around the World Party." It's not what you think - we got to drink like fifteen kinds of liquor from fifteen different countries. You know, in Mexico, we drank tequila; in Russia, we had vodka. It was AWESOME!!! And you're not going to believe it - I got a Star of David tattoo! I know I've kind of checked out from school already, but I've worked hard all semester, and it's time to chillax.

I've also been spending lots of time with Courtney. It's going to be really hard for us to be apart for all of winter vacation - do you think she can come with us on our New Year's family ski trip?

What time will you be here to pick me up on December 20th? If I still have work to do on my Psychology paper, you don't mind waiting around, do you?

Counting the days . . .
Adam

Growing Pains: What May Be Making Your ~~Baby~~ Young Adult Sick This Month

- Anxiety over preparations for final exams and final papers
- Adjustment to college exam schedule
- Sadness about leaving new friendships and/or love relationships
- Friendship tensions due to finals and living together for an extended period
- Extracurricular time strain, seasonal parties, end of the semester get-togethers, and religious activities
- Financial strain because of holiday gifts and for some, travel costs
- Anxiety or internal pressure for those who want to go home to see family and friends
- Doubts about academic competency or major
- Struggle between identity at college vs. identity among family and friends at home
- Final realization that they or others may not be able to return for second semester due to grades

Missing Holiday Events

My daughter will have final exams in another couple of weeks. Before that, she wants to come home for a few days to go to a friend's Christmas party, to attend a church service, and to do some holiday shopping. She thinks she can then go back to school to study and take her exams before coming home again for the winter break. I worry that her grades might suffer if she comes home before exams.

It can be hard for some students to be away from home around this time of the year. Holidays, such as Hanukkah, Kwanzaa and Christmas, take place around the same time that most universities schedule their exams, which makes it very difficult for students to participate in holiday events in the same ways they did when they were younger. Your daughter may be feeling like she needs to be part of the Christmas traditions and activities that have made the holiday special for her in past and, therefore, wants to come home before the semester is completely over.

Because final exam schedules are different from the normal semester schedules, first year students often experience the sense that they have more free time in their schedules during these final weeks. The exam period is spread out over one or two weeks; students can expect to have some days with no exams, and other days with one or two exams apiece.

At most universities, the final exam period is preceded by a study period, which can range from one day to upwards of one week of time when no classes are scheduled. This study period is intended to give students the opportunity to prepare for their final exams. First year students may be unaccustomed to such extended unscheduled blocks of time, and may perceive the study period and the days when they have no exams scheduled as free time to be spent with friends or, in your daughter's case, to use for Christmas shopping.

Your daughter says that she has the time to come home for a short stay before her final exams, but it might be the case that she isn't really clear on what work she has to do in preparation for her final exams. If she hasn't already done so, encourage your daughter to use a planner or calendar to write in all of her exams and all of the blocks of time she needs to commit to studying for each exam. This may help her get a more realistic picture of how much free time she really has, and she may see that she needs every minute she can get for studying.

You can also talk to your daughter about her reasons for wanting to come home. Is she feeling like she's missing out on Christmas traditions or not quite feeling the holiday spirit yet? There are ways that she can start getting involved in the holiday season while staying at school. You could send your daughter a care package with some holiday treats to share with her friends and some festive decorations (if she and her roommate agree that they'd like to decorate their room). Many universities plan events related to the holidays that their students celebrate. Your daughter can look into such events and activities to see if there are any she is interested in.

The university's chaplain or **campus ministry** can be an excellent resource for your daughter as well. They may have some religious services planned that will allow your daughter to celebrate the spiritual aspects of the holiday, if she'd like.

Another way to help your daughter get more comfortable with staying on campus during this time of the year would be to discuss the ways that she can celebrate the holiday once she gets home, and help her realize that it won't be too late to get into the Christmas spirit once she finishes exams and returns home for winter break. Perhaps you'll need to talk with your daughter about the fact that the days of sitting on Santa's lap are in the past. She might feel better knowing that the two of you will have lunch and make a shopping trip to the mall when she's home. This could become a new holiday tradition for the two of you.

The decision to come home is largely in your daughter's hands; perhaps further reflection will help her make an informed, rational decision about staying on campus or coming home early.

What to expect of your ~~baby~~ young adult in this situation:

* She will use a planner or calendar to write in all of her exams and all of the blocks of time she needs to commit to studying for each exam.
* She will find ways to celebrate the holiday season with her friends and/or her roommate.
* She will investigate what holiday activities and events are being planned on campus.
* She will contact the university chaplain or campus ministry about religious celebrations of the season.

TIME WITH A SIGNIFICANT OTHER

From what I can tell, my son and his new partner have been attached at the hip since October. He's planning to spend a lot of time and gas making the two hour trip to visit their family every weekend until

school's back in session. I think he's going to miss out on the rest and relaxation that he needs after his first semester in college. I'm also concerned that he'll be staying with a family that I don't really know anything about.

The relationships formed in the first semester can be quite intense, and may be a young adult's first experience with a serious girlfriend or boyfriend. Your son is apparently finding it difficult to imagine being apart from his new found love for any extended period of time, and this is normal. So, while you had your own ideas for how he would spend his winter break, your son has developed his own plan.

It's kind of like back when your son was a baby and you'd plan your afternoon with him: after his nice two hour nap, you'd take him for a walk, then meet some other babies and moms at the playground for a snack. Next thing you know, your baby wakes up an hour early, wants a snack right away, and to top it off, it's raining outside. From the start, your baby has shown you that your ideas and his don't always match.

Find an opportunity to talk to your son about winter break, preferably before he comes home. Help him to clarify what his plans and goals for the break may be. Does he want to work part-time and earn enough money to pay for his books next semester? Has he talked with his friends from high school about getting together? Does he want to be sure to have time to visit with his grandparents? He may need help from you in determining what he has time for and what his priorities are. Maybe regular trips to visit his partner will fit in with his other commitments, but maybe not.

You can also help your son by encouraging him to talk with his new flame about his ideas for break. He may have come up with this scheme for weekend visits without fully discussing it with them. They need to make sure that they are on the same page in terms of what they each want to do during winter break. Your son's partner also needs to have a conversation with their own parents to make sure that they are OK with him coming to visit.

Consider suggesting to your son some alternative ways for him to spend time with his partner. Maybe they can each drive an hour and meet for a date in the middle somewhere. Or maybe your son's significant other can come to visit at your house for a day or two. This would give you the chance to get to know them better, as well.

If your son does make a weekend visit to their house, try to set aside some time to talk to him about his experience there when he gets back. Do some probing to find out a bit more about the way they spent their time, and about whether he enjoyed their time together. Before he goes back to visit again, help him to make an honest assessment of how well the trip went. He may say something like, "It was nice and all, but the two hour drive each way is too long to make again next weekend" or "Their family is great, but I can't stand their cat. I sneezed the whole time I was there." If you talk with your son without being critical of his decisions, he'll hopefully make a decision about future visits that is rational and smart for him.

It's understandable for you to feel concern about your son spending time with a family that you do not know. It's hard, because you can't just pick up the phone and call his partner's parents like you did when arranging play dates years ago. You are going to have to rely on your son's judgment when it comes to the time spent with their family. One way that college students learn and grow is by experiencing how other people live, through study abroad trips, living with roommates and visiting college friends at their homes. As long as his partner's family's lifestyle isn't contradictory to your family's morals and values, you can chalk up time spent there as a learning experience for your son.

That said, continue your family's conversations about values and beliefs, and continue to help your son put his values and beliefs into action in his relationship with his significant other.

What to expect of your ~~baby~~ young adult in this situation:

* He will think about and clarify his ideas and goals for winter break.
* He will talk with his partner about his plans for break to make sure that they are on the same page.
* He will consider alternative ways for him to spend time with his partner, such as meeting one another at a halfway point or having them visit him at home.

* If he does decide to visit, he will ask his partner to talk with their parents first and make sure that they are OK with him coming to visit.
* If he does visit, he will make an honest assessment of how well the trip went before making any further visits.

Religious Holiday Celebrations

We are Jewish and have never celebrated any of the religious holidays at this time of the year. My daughter is feeling very uncomfortable with the intensity of holiday celebrations she sees around campus. For example, her residence hall suite has organized a gift swap, and has set up a Christmas tree in the common room. What should she do?

It sounds like your daughter is on a campus that is steeped in Christian religious traditions. On the surface, it may seem like she is the only student who practices a different religion. Chances are, there are a good number of students on campus who are either Jewish or who come from a variety of other religious traditions. If your daughter is a practicing Jew, there is an international organization called **Hillel** which can be found on most college campuses.

The formal name of the organization is *Hillel: The Foundation for Jewish Campus Life* and is the largest Jewish campus organization in the world. According to Hillel's website, the organization's stated mission is "to enrich the lives of Jewish students so that they may enrich the Jewish people and the world" (hillel.org). In practical terms, campus Hillel foundations engage Jewish students in religious, cultural, artistic, and community-service activities.

Your daughter may be interested in joining Hillel in order to spend time with students who come from similar backgrounds. If she doesn't care to join a group based on religious affiliation, but merely wants to voice her discomfort and concerns about the campus's focus on one particular religious tradition, there are a number of approaches she could take. First, she may want to speak with her RA to get a sense of the campus climate. The majority of college campuses are well aware that their student bodies consist of young adults from diverse religious, ethnic, and cultural backgrounds. Departments and programs on many campuses are organized around the philosophy that students from all backgrounds need to understand the concepts of cooperation, collaboration, and inclusion relative to religion, race, color, gender, sexual orientation, national origin, or disability. A department of this type may be called the **multicultural center.** Common programming on some campuses is focused on diversity awareness or diversity training where workshops or educational programming are likely to be offered out of some type of multicultural center. A resident assistant or her first-year experience instructor should be able to point her in the direction of this campus resource.

What to expect of your ~~baby~~ young adult in this situation:

* She will find out about the Hillel organization on her campus if she wishes to join a group based on religious affiliation.
* She will speak to her RA to get a sense of the campus climate.
* She will do some research to determine the forum on her campus to voice her concerns.
* She will talk to her first-year experience instructor to learn about the Multicultural Center on campus or to learn more about the campus diversity programming.

Apathetic About Going Home

Now that the semester is almost over, I would have thought that my son would be excited to be coming home for a month. Instead, he seems rather hesitant about living at home again. He doesn't seem like himself anymore. What gives?

Remember, if your son is the traditional age for a first-year college student, then he is eighteen or nineteen years old. This puts him dead center into what psychologists call the "late adolescent stage of development." What does that mean? Well, during the transition from high school to college, your son is simultaneously experiencing a psychological transition from adolescence to young adulthood. This developmental stage is typically marked by a search for identity. In other words, your babies are trying to 'find themselves." Remember when they first looked in the mirror, and you saw their little faces change when they had that discovery, "Hey mom, look!!! That's my face in the glass!!!" Right now, they are spending a lot of time looking at the reflection in the mirror and trying all over again to figure out who that person looking back at them really is. The quest for individual identity is common at this age and stage. Young adults are trying to figure out, "Who am I?" and "What should I be when I grow up?"

When your son was living at home with you, you helped shape his identity. As a member of your family, he had a ready-made group where he always "fit in." During the adolescent stage, peers are stronger influences, and now it is up to your son, all on his own, to figure out whom he fits in with best. If he is still trying to solidify his identity, this can be a real challenge. So, what do adolescents sometimes do to figure this out? They may literally "try on" different identities to figure out what or who they feel most comfortable with.

Consider this scenario: let's say your son was raised traditionally Catholic and never ate meat on Fridays. Suddenly, he is sharing meals with students from a variety of religious traditions. He has been enjoying steak regularly on Fridays throughout the entire semester. He reasons that the friend he met from Kazakhstán not only eats meat on Fridays, but he also discovers that Kazakhs eat horses. Your son feels enlightened, and figures, well, what's the harm of eating steak on a Friday, then? Perhaps the young woman in his comparative religion class, after reading about Hinduism, decides to become a vegetarian. In college, young adults try out a lot of new things. The point is, adolescents will not only experiment with their religious ideologies, but they will also test many aspects of their identities: the way they dress, their likes and dislikes, hobbies, who they spend time with, their political affiliations, how they adorn themselves (piercings, tattoos and all) and the list goes on.

To answer your question, in your son's search for his "self," he may feel concerned that his "home self" and "school self" are different, and perhaps you won't like this new school self or understand it. This stage of development can be confusing for parents and babies alike. On one hand, your son may be calling you at home with a dilemma like, "I hate my roommate; you have to tell me what to do." They'll demand you make decisions for them out of the fear of making their own decisions. In the same breath you will hear them say, "You can't tell me what to do; you don't know anything!!!"

So, it's entirely possible that your son is steeped in the confusion of this complex stage of development; however, there is also the possibility that he has simply enjoyed the unbridled freedom he's had during his time away from home, and he is wondering what restrictions he may face when he moves back in with you. Let's face it, he has been allowed to come and go as he pleases for the last three months.

The question for you is, have you asked him about the noticeable change in his demeanor? See if you can find out where he is coming from and try not to put him on the defensive. You might say, "I am really look-ing forward to having you at home again, but the last couple of times we've talked, you don't seem as excited for your break as I am. Can you tell me what's going on?" If he says, "nothing," leave it alone . . . for now. When he does get home, take some time to observe his behavior. If you are still worried, raise your concerns again. This time, you may approach it as a conversation about "renegotiating" the rules at home since you recognize that he has spent a considerable amount of time away and has handled it responsibly. If you are concerned about the different school self that you see, ask your son what lead to his decision to change his political affilia-tion, his diet, or why he decided to get a tattoo or piercing?

Try not to react too harshly to the differences you might observe. Adolescents may try on many different selves during this age and stage, but research suggests that though they will change (grow up), they usually circle back around to their roots and the solid grounding you provided for them just like when you supported them through their first steps.

What to expect of your ~~baby~~ young adult in this situation:

- He will treat you with respect when he is living at home.
- He will discuss with you his thoughts and feelings about the changes you are observing.
- He will be willing to listen to your concerns and attempt to understand why you may be feeling disappointed by his lack of enthusiasm about coming home.
- If he seems reluctant talk to you about his confusion (that is if he is indeed confused), he will talk with someone in the counseling office at school to sort out his feelings.

MONEY CONCERNS

Now that the semester is over, my daughter is very low on money. She's now upset about the holidays because she didn't save any money to buy gifts for her family and friends.

Well, this is a tough one. You may think of one of Granny's old adages: either "money doesn't grow on trees" or "necessity is the mother of invention." Let's take the first one. Do you need to have the old "money doesn't grow on trees" talk with your daughter? Why is it that she doesn't have any money left after the first semester? Did you talk finances with her before she left for school? What were the expectations you set up as a family? What happened during the semester that left her "broke," with no money to purchase holiday gifts? Was it because of poor financial planning on her part? Frivolous spending? Did she have unexpected expenses that came up that she didn't account for? Did college and its expenses just plain old cost more than she (and perhaps you) anticipated?

A number of things might be going on. Back to this idea of diversity. Again, your daughter is meeting other young adults from a wide variety of backgrounds. One component of diversity is socioeconomic class. Indeed, she is meeting students from different backgrounds in this respect. Yes, she will come in contact with the students on financial aid struggling to make ends meet, but her roommate could be the "rich kid" who can afford to go shopping every week at the mall to keep up with the latest fashion trends. Or maybe the people she is hanging out with can afford to eat out a lot or have discretionary money to spend on entertainment like going to the movies. Is it that your daughter was trying to "keep up with the Jones'?" Perhaps she spent all of her money to keep up? It's very hard for young adults to say no to requests for invitations when they are trying to fit in socially. Find out from your daughter what the issues are. What led her to breaking the bank, or worse yet, getting into some debt? In the case of getting herself into debt, you may have to use "the money doesn't grow on trees" talk. If it was the inability to say "no," and she went along with the crowd to keep up, the old, "would you jump off a bridge just because all of your friends did?" talk may have to be revisited.

If, on the other hand, by all accounts she seemed to have handled the money responsibly, and it just wasn't enough to meet the expenses, here's where "necessity is the mother of invention" comes into play. Although you may tell her that relatives and friends should be empathetic to the plight of the poor, starving college student (and they should indeed understand the sacrifice your family is making to provide a good education), she may still want to give gifts like she always has. Since she has no money, you might suggest that she gives her time to her relatives and friends. She could create a coupon book that offers her services. Maybe she could babysit for a relative, help her grandparents with grocery shopping or clean her aunt's house. She could bake cookies with her little cousins. She may want to volunteer at a charity in someone's name. Perhaps someone in her circle has had cancer. She could present the promise of completing a walk-a-thon in their honor. She could make gifts. A family photograph or photo collage is always an appreciated gift. She could look through her old pictures and see what might work. There are many things she could do that won't cost money...only her time.

You can be sure that during winter break, college students have plenty of time. A typical semester break is four to six weeks. If she doesn't have a formal job, there are lots of projects she could complete with all of that free time. The other solution, of course, is for her to work over semester break.

Given that it is holiday time, many places look for seasonal employees. So yes, "necessity is the mother of invention." It's time for your daughter to be inventive!!

What to expect of your ~~baby~~ young adult in this situation:

* She will be willing to engage in a frank discussion with you about her spending habits.
* If she was frivolous, she will "come clean" about why she doesn't have any money for her holiday gifts.
* She will investigate creative ways to give her time in lieu of pricey gifts.
* She will investigate the feasibility of working over break.

ALCOHOL IMPACTING GRADES

My son has checked out for the semester. He is doing very poorly in all of his classes, and is no longer doing any school work. I suspect that he has been drinking too much this semester, and this has probably caused him to fail his classes. Is it too late for him to turn things around?

There's some urgency in this situation, and your son needs to take action immediately.

It might be too late for your son to salvage his grades this semester, but maybe not. It's really important that your son find out how he is doing in all of his classes. He needs to meet with each of his professors, be frank about what's been going on, and discuss whether it is possible for him to get a passing grade.

Some professors may be willing to work with your son to help him get caught up and to pass, but it is his responsibility to initiate these conversations. If the professors do provide him with an opportunity to pass the course, your son must be willing to do *everything* they ask of him. You can encourage your son to visit the **learning center** to see if they can support him in completing his work.

Your son should also meet with his **academic advisor** as soon as possible. The academic advisor can provide your son with the information on university policies that will impact his situation and can explain to your son the various options he has when it comes to his grades. For example, he may be able to withdraw without penalty from a class that he doesn't have a chance of passing. He may also be able to get an extension to complete the work at a later date. And, if he can't earn passing grades in some or all of his courses, his academic advisor can help him understand how this will impact his course loads in subsequent semesters.

If he is not going to be able to earn passing grades in any of his classes, your son needs to talk to you and his advisor about his options. You'll need to decide with him whether he should remain on campus until the end of the semester; it may make more sense for him to return home immediately, rather than to wait until classes are over.

While your son is working on trying to get his academic life in order, you will need to have some serious conversations with him about what's gone wrong this semester. And it's a good thing now, that unlike when he was a baby, he has the vocabulary to tell you what's going on. He may not be fully honest with you about this, so like when he was little, you may have to help him along and pull some teeth in your talks, and try to read between the lines. Have he and his friends been drinking during evenings throughout the week, and then missing classes the following mornings? Has he been drinking during times when most students have been at class? What other factors besides alcohol have impacted his grades this semester? For example, if he is upset about the break-up with his girlfriend from high school, that may be impacting his grades, and may be leading him to drink more as well. These discussions with your son will help you both make appropriate decisions about his academic career.

It also will be important to assess whether you think you son's drinking is posing a health risk to him; if so, this is one of the few times that we'd recommend *you* contact university staff members yourself, rather than simply encouraging your son to do so. It may also be helpful to speak with one or two of your son's closest friends at college to gauge whether they have similar concerns. If so, you could recruit them to encourage your son to seek help. In either case, you can contact your son's academic advisor, the health services department, or the head of the residential life department. Explain your concerns about your son's physical well-being and request that they intervene with him. If you think that your son's drinking is endangering him, be prepared to bring him home.

If your son is having trouble emotionally, whether in relation to his drinking or other factors, strongly encourage him to seek help from counseling services. If there is a chance for him to pass his classes this semester, the staff at the **counseling services** office can help him manage his stress appropriately. They can also talk to him about his use of alcohol and assist him in developing healthier habits.

When your son returns home for winter break, you will have the opportunity for some face to face discussions of his situation. This is the right time to learn his view of what went wrong over the past semester, and to determine whether he has the ability and desire to change his behaviors. He may sound like he's in denial or doesn't seem to really grasp what the big deal is: "I was just doing what everyone else was doing, but my classes were harder than theirs." Or he may express regret, without any real understanding of what he needs to change: "I was just out of control this first semester, being away from home for the first time. Next semester will be different." Maybe he'll have thought through what happened over recent months, and be ready to take action: "That's it! No more studying in my room where everyone's partying. From now on, I'll be at the library every night after dinner."

In any case, it will be important to talk to him about what concrete changes he plans to make if he returns to college for second semester. While he is at home, help him face up to his final grades from the first semester. He very likely will have a low GPA (grade point average), and may be on academic probation (typically in college, students with a GPA below C- are placed on academic probation) in the second semester. Help him develop some goals and a game plan to attain these goals. If he seems unwilling or unable to develop defined, achievable goals and strategies to reach them, he may not be ready for another semester at college.

What to expect of your ~~baby~~ young adult in this situation:

- He will meet with all of his professors to determine whether he can pass their courses.
- He will meet with his academic advisor to discuss his options with his current and future courses.
- If he is having emotional problems, he will meet with someone from the university's counseling services office.
- He will discuss with you what happened during the semester, and develop a concrete plan to achieve his goals if he returns to college for the second semester.

STEP-BY-STEP . . .
COUNSELING SERVICES: CONSULTING THE SPECIALISTS FOR A COLICKY ~~BABY~~ YOUNG ADULT

Whether or not your baby was afflicted many years ago, you likely remember a condition called colic. According to the Mayo Clinic, colic is when an otherwise healthy baby cries or screams frequently for extended periods without any discernible reason. The amount of crying differs between babies and doctors still have not conclusively agreed on the cause or treatment. So, what to do if all of a sudden your otherwise healthy young adult starts crying more than is typical for their temperaments? What's the cause and what to do to treat this condition?

As already mentioned, college is a time of big changes. These changes are exciting, but for some, they can be challenging and confusing. The cause of your young adult's distress could just be a touch of the first-year blues, or maybe even mild depression. Incoming students can expect to have an adjustment period, but what if that typical homesickness seems to last a little too long? What to do to treat it? If your young adult is crying all the time and can't seem to tell you why, a college counseling center can help them figure it out.

The majority of colleges and universities have counseling centers to help students effectively manage typical developmental tasks (adjusting to living away from home), situational crises (a break up of a significant relationship), and personal problems (the onset of an eating disorder) that may interfere with their day to day lives. In other words, colleges and universities anticipate that your babies may need a little help "coping with their colic" and understand that the severity of the condition will vary among students. Counseling centers provide a private confidential place to sort out a wide variety of issues that may prevent your babies from having a productive, emotionally healthy college experience. You can expect that if your young adult chooses to seek out counseling on their campuses, all conversations will be kept confidential within professional and legal guidelines.

The following are some common issues for which students seek out counseling on college campuses (from Bryant University Counseling Services):

* Anxiety
* Depression
* Alcohol/substance use & abuse
* Self-esteem
* Relationships
* Body image
* Loneliness
* Family issues
* Eating concerns
* Grief/loss
* Roommate issues
* Sexuality
* Time management
* Adjustment issues
* Identity Issues
* Sexual Assault

Many colleges and universities offer a wide variety of services through their counseling centers such as crisis intervention, individual counseling, group counseling, brief psychotherapy, psychological assessment, referrals for psychiatric assessment, and mental health screening.

You may be concerned about your colicky babies and worried about whether they will seek out counseling services if they need it. The good news is that effective counseling centers typically do a lot of outreach education. They may offer workshops on substance abuse and eating disorders to mention a few. These departments may partner with their campus wellness programs to offer educational programs on healthy eating, for example. Many counseling centers offer alcohol education programming. These departments know when National Depression Screening Day takes place.

Effective counseling centers consult and collaborate with faculty, staff, administration and other university departments to promote healthy student development and a healthy environment for students. Counseling centers work with other departments to raise students' awareness about potential risks to their emotional, academic, and social health.

Step-By-Step . . .
Campus Ministries and Religious Groups: Not Just for the Anointed ~~Babies~~ Young Adults

Now that your young adults are away from home, decisions related to their spiritual and religious lives have shifted almost fully onto their shoulders. No longer do they have you to wake them up on Sunday mornings for church services, or to help them remember that they need to fast for one of the high holidays. These responsibilities are now up to your young adult, but there are people at college who can help.

Most universities have chaplains and religious groups with a campus presence. The names of the groups vary widely, depending on the university and the religious affiliation. Some groups are sponsored and supported by the university administration, while others are student-run organizations. The religious groups are often affiliated with a specific religion, but some universities do have non-denominational spiritual advisors and chaplains.

Often, a religious group's presence on campus is determined by the make-up of a university's student body and/or nearby community. For instance, a university that has many Jewish students in attendance will likely have a Jewish chaplain on staff. But, at a university with very few Catholic students, there may be no chaplain or religious group dedicated specifically to those students.

University chaplains, ministries, and student groups offer students the opportunity to practice their religious beliefs. Depending on the university, they may have religious services specifically for students, or as part of a parish or group from the wider community. In addition to religious services, these ministry individuals and groups help students to perform community service, to receive religious or spiritual counseling, to connect with other members of a religious community and to learn more about religious faiths.

These groups typically do not require that students be practicing the religion to take part in the activities and services they offer. Often, students learn about their friends' faiths by attending religious activities with them. This doesn't mean that your son or daughter is going to convert to a new religion – it's just part of having new experiences and learning about new cultures and ways of thinking.

Your young adult can find out more about the campus ministry, chaplains and student religious groups on campus by checking out the campus website. If there is not a group dedicated to the religion that your family practices, you can recommend that they talk to the campus-appointed chaplain or student religious group advisor. That individual may be able to help your son or daughter connect with an affiliated group from the wider community that does practice your religion.

CHAPTER 6

January

● ● ●

January 25th

Dear Mom and Dad,

I'm back at school safe and sound. I miss you guys! Especially the food! The food here stinks, and I've already broken my New Year's Resolution to eat healthier. All the healthy options in the dining hall are disgusting. I've been skipping the dining hall altogether, and spending all the money I earned working over break on pizzas and fast food.

So, everyone else on my floor is planning to pledge that sorority this semester, even Jen's new roommate Erin. I think I will too, because I don't want to be the only one not doing it. I never really wanted to be part of a sorority, but I don't want to lose my friends. I know you want me to focus on pulling up my GPA this semester, but that's not my top priority right now.

Love you,
Johanna

Growing Pains: What May Be Giving Your ~~Baby~~ Young Adult Diaper Rash This Month

* Readjusting to living away from home after winter break, including a sense of relief or possible bouts with homesickness

- Considering joining a sorority or fraternity
- Completing financial aid paperwork for sophomore year
- Seeking a fresh start; trying to change some bad habits from first semester
- Needing to pay off debt accumulated during holidays and time with friends
- Trying to lose weight from first semester and winter break activities
- Adjusting to the addition of some new students in the residence hall, or the loss of friends who may not have returned

NEW ADDITION TO RESIDENCE HALL

My son is not happy to be back at college. He was really close with all of the students on his residence hall floor. But over break, one of his friends moved back home and is now commuting, and another transferred to a different school. Now there are two new students living on his floor, and he says that he doesn't like his living situation anymore. I don't want this to ruin his experience.

Each semester typically brings changes in residence halls. This creates a challenge for your son as he must continue to adjust to living away from home among his peers. He really enjoyed his living experience last semester, and thinks that nothing can top it, especially since some of the people who were important to him are no longer there.

You can recommend that your son talk to his **RA** about the changes. Many resident assistants recognize the need to regroup and reorient the students they are responsible for, and make an effort to ease the transition, both for the new students on the floor and for the returners. RAs often plan events at this time of the year that allow the students to get together and establish, or re-establish, connections.

Once he gets to know them better, your son may find that one or both of the new students on his floor are great guys who fit in well with the already formed group. He may have had the experience at some point in his life of meeting someone that he didn't like initially, and then finding that person to be a great friend. You may be able to remind him of such past experiences, and encourage him to take the time to get to know the new residents, and to give them a chance.

Then again, it may turn out that your son really doesn't enjoy the company of these guys. If that's the case, then he can turn to his other friends and dorm mates. It sounds like he has some other good friends on his floor already, and just because his other buddy is now commuting doesn't mean that they cannot continue their friendship.

The second semester is also a good time to start branching out a bit. Now that he has had one semester to experience the rigors of college, your son may be in a better position to get involved with campus activities if he hasn't already. He may want to join a club or participate in new on-campus activities. This will give him a chance to get to know more people that share his interests. He can talk to his RA or visit the Student Involvement Office to find out more about clubs and campus involvement.

What to expect of your ~~baby~~ young adult in this situation:

* He will take some time to get to know the new students on his floor.
* He will talk to his RA about the new living environment.
* He will look into other ways to meet students, including joining clubs and campus activities.

JOINING A FRATERNITY OR SORORITY

At my son's school, fraternity pledging is done during the spring semester. My son never really expressed interest in joining a fraternity before, but now he is planning to do so. I'm nervous. He got average grades last semester, but I'm afraid his academics may slip. And what about all those hazing horror stories?

This is one of those times with your young adult when you wish you could choose his friends for him, or forbid him from hanging out with people you may not approve of. However, fraternities and sororities can be a great experience for students. They often help students develop life-long friendships, leadership and teamwork skills, a sense of community action, and future professional connections. But there are other aspects of fraternities and sororities that are certainly a cause for concern. For example, recent studies have found that fraternity and sorority members drink more frequently and drink in greater quantities than other students (Barry, 2007). Frequent, heavy drinking by college students is linked with lower grades, injuries, sexual assaults, and arrests. Some data suggests higher frequency of drug use by fraternity and sorority members as well (Addiction Center, 2016).

The pledge period can be especially demanding. During this period of weeks or months, the new fraternity members undergo an initiation in which they learn the history and rules of the fraternity, establish bonds with other fraternity members, and demonstrate their commitment to the group. The structure and requirements of the initiation vary widely among fraternities and among colleges.

Initiation can include activities that are fun for participants, involve team building, and challenge new members appropriately. However, when the activities required for membership are degrading or dangerous, they are defined as hazing. Many colleges have made efforts to eliminate hazing, but it still happens in many fraternities and sororities.

While fraternities are often quite secretive about the pledging and initiation experience, your son should try to find out what he can about what will be expected of him. Fraternities aim to recruit new members, and will make existing members available to answer questions. Your son can also consider talking with friends and acquaintances, particularly sophomores, juniors and seniors who may have observed other students' experiences during the pledge period in previous years. His **RA** may be a good resource for such information. There is usually a university staff person who oversees the fraternities and sororities on campus. If your son needs more information about fraternity membership, he can contact the **Greek life coordinator** at his college.

Once he has done some of this research, discuss with your son what he knows about the fraternity, including its requirements, benefits, drawbacks and initiation practices. Ask him to consider whether the fraternity's values and expectations are in line with his, in terms of time commitment, academics, socializing, money and other areas. For example, if your son is expected to pay a large amount of money in fraternity dues, is that feasible? Or, if the expectation is that all fraternity members must live in the fraternity house, and your son was planning on moving in with other friends in his sophomore year, how will he reconcile this? If he found the first semester of college a challenge, how will he manage to get his work done effectively during the pledge period? While joining a fraternity is his choice, you can help your son consider these questions. Please be aware that your son may only have a few days to declare his intention to pledge a fraternity, so time is of the essence for him to consider all aspects of this important decision.

If your son is going to succeed academically while pledging, he will need to work hard and stay organized. His fraternity may have rules and support systems in place to ensure members get their course work done, but there are many other demands on their time. You can encourage him to use a calendar or planner to track all of the fraternity and academic requirements of the semester. He should set aside specific times for his academic work, and will need to replace this time if it is unexpectedly taken up with pledging activities. If he needs help with getting organized, he can meet with a learning specialist at his college's academic support center; if he struggles with a specific course, he should inquire at the academic support center about tutoring for that class before he gets over his head.

As the pledge period progresses over the semester, continue to talk with your son about his experiences with the initiation. Do not be surprised if he is unwilling to share details, as secrecy is often expected of fraternity members. But, be observant of his manner, emotions, and physical appearance; if you notice signs of sleep deprivation, stress, or anything out of the ordinary, mention this to him. He may open up a bit, and allow you a chance to offer some suggestions for how to handle certain situations.

What to expect of your ~~baby~~ young adult in this situation:

    ❋   He will make an informed decision about joining a fraternity by talking to as many people as he can about the fraternity's practices and reputation on campus. Consider talking with upperclassmen, his RA, and/or the Greek life advisor on campus.

* If he chooses to join a fraternity, he will maintain strong grades by staying organized with his time and seeking help when needed.

* If he experiences excessive stress, or if he experiences initiation activities that are degrading or dangerous, he will discuss it with you or someone else he trusts.

HOMESICKNESS?

My daughter was never homesick last fall. She loved college and seemed to have a great time the entire semester. Now, she's sounding down in the dumps, and says she misses being home with all of her friends. She told me the other day that she doesn't know if she has the energy to make it through another semester. Is she homesick, or is this something else?

Yes, it's possible that your daughter is homesick, even though she's already been at college for an entire semester. She may have been caught up in all the excitement and newness of the first semester, and didn't really see what she was missing until she was home with everyone for winter break. There's something about college right now that is making home the preferable location for your daughter. You and she need to figure out what that is, so that she can have another successful semester.

There are different areas of the college experience that can cause stress or reluctance to return to campus. For example, academically, your daughter may be dreading a specific class that she is required to take this semester, or she may have realized that she doesn't really care for her chosen major after all. Socially, your daughter and her roommate may have left for break after a big argument; or, after spending time with her friends at home, she may have realized that the set of college friends she formed in the first semester aren't really the people she wants to hang around with.

Whatever is causing her lack of enthusiasm, there are campus resources that are available to help support her return. The first person she can talk to is her **RA**, who can help direct her to the appropriate resource. If she is reconsidering her major, she may want to talk to her academic advisor and/or the career center. If she wants to branch out socially, she can visit the student involvement center.

If she seems to be unenthusiastic about every area of her life, is withdrawing, or is consistently unable to accomplish daily tasks, your daughter may be experiencing depression. She should speak with someone in the **counseling center** immediately. If you have concerns about your daughter's mental health, be sure to address this with her immediately.

What to expect of your ~~baby~~ young adult in this situation:

+ She will identify what is causing her lack of enthusiasm for her return to college by talking with you or someone else she trusts.
+ Once she is aware of why she is feeling homesick, she will speak with her RA about appropriate resources on campus.
+ She will follow through with suggestions that her RA gives her regarding campus resources.
+ If she continues to feel sad about being away from home, she will speak with someone in counseling services.

Financial Aid

My son contacted me because he just found out that he needs to get his financial aid forms in as soon as possible. He and I are both nervous about whether we can afford to send him back to the same college next semester. Is there anything he should be doing to win over the financial aid people?

If a student receives financial aid, they must reapply every year. According the FAFSA website, it is important to know the deadlines for the aid that your son will be applying for. Deadlines for state aid vary by state. Often the deadlines for school aid may also be quite early in the year. Some other programs award aid based on the information filed in the FAFSA (Free Application for Federal Student Aid), and these programs may have early deadlines as well.

Some universities and states award aid on a first-come, first-served basis; be sure to find out what the process is for your son's institution and for your home state, if applicable. Creating a calendar can be a good way to make sure all of the deadlines are met. If you or your son have questions related to the FAFSA, consider meeting with the financial aid office before submitting, but be aware that time is ticking. The federal government's FAFSA website is also an excellent resource for further information.

Once the application is submitted, your son will likely receive notice from the financial aid office regarding the aid he has been awarded. From there, you and your son will be able to follow up by meeting with a representative from the university's financial aid office. The financial aid office staff can help you better understand the aid offered, and can provide additional options for aid, which may include scholarships or loans. The earlier you know how much financial aid your son will receive, the better it will be for the decision-making process should the cost be too high for your family to bear. In future semesters, it may be a good idea to work on the financial aid requirements before your son returns to college after break.

What to expect of your ~~baby~~ young adult in this situation:

- He will work with you to make a list of questions that you both have regarding financial aid and tuition.
- He will make an appointment with the financial aid office to get answers to the questions you developed and to find out what he needs to do to apply for financial aid.
- He will explore scholarships and other funding options to supplement existing financial aid.
- He will use a calendar to track all important deadlines related to financial aid and tuition.

PULLING UP GRADES THIS SEMESTER
My daughter barely squeaked by in her first semester at college. Now she's back at school for another semester, but I am not sensing that

she's doing anything different. She just said that she's going to "study more," but I know for a fact that she has a semester-long research project that she is already behind on. I think she needs a clearer plan of action, but I'm not sure what that is.

Remember when your daughter was in elementary school? Each year, there would be a new classroom, a new teacher, and maybe a new group of classmates. It was nice to have a fresh start each year. The nice thing about college is that this opportunity for a fresh start comes around twice a year, with the start of each new semester or term (at some universities, there may even be trimesters or quarters). So, this is a great chance for your daughter to improve academically and there are things that she can do to avoid squandering this opportunity.

It does sound like your daughter needs clearer plans and goals for the semester to make the most of this fresh start. This is important in general, but especially necessary when there is a major project to work on. Your daughter needs to make sure she is organized and on top of all the assignments she has for the semester. Now is a good time for her to review all of her syllabi from her courses, and get all of her assignments, exams, papers and presentations listed in her planner. If your daughter has difficulty with these types of organizational tasks, you can recommend that she meet with a **learning specialist** in the university's learning center.

The learning specialist can also help your daughter pinpoint any academic skills she may need to develop further. It's more than just studying for longer hours; it's about studying and working more effectively. Perhaps your daughter needs to master some college-level reading skills or learn how to take notes more efficiently. Encourage her to meet with a learning specialist to help her get on track.

When a student has a large research project, like your daughter's, it's great for them to build that project into their schedule, so that they aren't overwhelmed with trying to get it done at the end of the semester. Encourage your daughter to break down this project into smaller, manageable pieces with set due dates. These smaller tasks may include: doing library research, interviewing an expert, and developing a survey. Each of them on their own is not as bad as trying to do all these tasks at once.

For assistance with this type of research project, there are some great resources on campus. First, your daughter should develop a good working relationship with her professor for the course. She should visit the professor during **office hours,** and discuss her ideas for the project. Her professor is likely to give her additional guidance if your daughter shows that she is making an effort.

Another excellent resource for research projects is the library. University libraries of today are quite different in some ways to those of previous generations. There are more resources available to students and, as a result, the act of conducting research has become more sophisticated. Most universities recognize this, and the **reference and research librarians** are more likely to actively assist students in learning how to find the sources that they need. Suggest that your daughter make a visit to the library and speak with a librarian about her project.

What to expect of your ~~baby~~ young adult in this situation:

* She will review her syllabi and use a calendar to keep track of assignments, papers, exams and presentations.
* She will break down her research project into manageable tasks, and set deadlines to complete these tasks.
* She will meet with a learning specialist to work on developing any academic skills that she struggles with.
* She will meet with her professor and visit the library for additional support on her research project.

Freshman 15

Even though my daughter has always been on the slim side, she came home from her first semester in college noticeably heavier. She said she wasn't happy with her Freshman 15 (actually, Freshman 12 in her case), but over break, she didn't make any real effort to lose weight. Now that she's back at college, she's determined to get back to an appropriate weight for her. She's embarrassed and says her clothes don't fit anymore. Is it possible to lose weight at college?

The infamous Freshman 15 refers to the fifteen pounds a student is said to gain in their first year. So you thought you were done talking about your baby's weight with the pediatrician. In reality, many students do gain weight in their first months in college, but typically they gain less than 15 pounds on average.

There are several reasons that lead to this phenomenon. The dining hall food is different from the food that students eat at home. There are usually tons of options; students can choose what they'd like to eat from a huge variety, and they can eat as much as they'd like. For example, in many households, dessert is only served at special-occasion meals like birthdays and holidays. In the university dining hall, students can have dessert at just about every meal. And while most dining halls do offer more nutritious options (like salad bars), there is no one there to encourage your daughter to eat a healthy, balanced meal.

A college student's daily schedule can also lead to weight gain. Many students skip breakfast because they sleep in, or they just don't want to go to the dining hall in the morning. Skipping breakfast has been linked to weight gain, perhaps because this leads to hunger later in the day. If your daughter skips breakfast, she may be eating too much at lunch and dinner, or snacking between meals. College students are also notoriously up late, when less healthy take-out and vending machine food can be tempting. Eating later at night and then going to sleep soon afterward does not give the body the adequate time to burn off these calories.

One other major factor in weight gain for college students is alcohol consumption. Students often do not think about the liquid calories in their diets. Beer or other alcoholic drinks not only add unneeded calories to a student's diet, but they also may lead to additional unmindful eating. Once the party is over, it is not uncommon for students to order pizza or get delivery from a late-night restaurant.

If you get the sense that your daughter doesn't know that these factors may lead to weight gain, if she seems open to listening, you may want to share this information with her. There are many websites and articles just for college students that you can suggest that she check out. Her own college may even have information on its website.

Despite all of these nutritional challenges, it is possible for students to lose weight when they are at college. Your daughter should take a close look at her eating habits. At the beginning of a change in eating lifestyle, it is helpful to keep an eating log. Your daughter can use a phone app to log not only what she eats, but the time of the day, the location, and her hunger level at the times she eats. This may help her identify patterns in her eating, including some of those mentioned above, like having dessert at every dining hall meal or eating pizza during study breaks. From there, she can identify some habits that she'd like to target for change. Some strategies she will want to consider include:

* Choosing fewer and/or healthier items at all-you-can eat dining halls
* Eating breakfast
* Eliminating or limiting alcohol consumption
* Eliminating or limiting late-night eating

Of course, the other major component of weight loss is exercise. Often, with the other time commitments of college life, students cut exercise out of their daily routines. Or other students may have never really needed an exercise routine before. Perhaps your daughter got a healthy dose of physical activity by playing high school sports. As she begins implementing a new eating routine, she should also consider ways to get more physical activity.

There are many ways she can build exercise into her routine. Many colleges have a gym or other workout facilities. Some even have workout rooms in residence halls. These are often free for students. If there is no campus gym, there may be a gym within walking or driving distance. If your daughter doesn't like this type of exercise, she may prefer walking or running, or doing workout videos. Any of these activities are possible to do with friends. Perhaps she can find some other people in her residence hall who want to work out together.

Many colleges offer intramural sports or recreational sports, which are another fun way to get more active. In intramural or recreational sports leagues, groups of students get together to form teams. Teams are made up of friends, residence hall residents, classmates, club members, or any other combination of students. These teams sign up to compete in a league sort against other teams. Some typical intramural and recreational sports include volleyball, basketball, and soccer. Some colleges have a wide variety of these leagues. If your daughter is interested in this, she can check with her RA, or visit her college's gym or wellness center for more information.

Your daughter should choose a physical activity that she enjoys (or hates least!) and that fits with her schedule and lifestyle. She should schedule her activities just as she does her other commitments, like classes and club meetings. If she can build physical activity into her daily and weekly routines, she will not only succeed in losing weight, but she will be less likely to fall ill and will have an excellent outlet for stress.

Many colleges have staff available that can help your daughter with becoming healthier. You can recommend that she find out if there is a health educator or nutritionist that she can meet with to discuss her goal of losing weight. These staff members can help her examine her current food choices and activity level, can suggest some helpful strategies, and can support her as she works toward her goal of a more healthy college lifestyle.

Your daughter's college may also have trainers available to work with students that want to develop an exercise routine. Trainers may be professionals or other students with expertise in this area. They can show her the right ways to approach her exercise activities.

What to expect of your ~~baby~~ young adult in this situation:

* She will monitor her eating habits for a couple of weeks. Then, she will make some specific changes in terms of what, when, where and why she eats.
* She will find a physical activity that she enjoys and build it into her daily and/or weekly routine.
* She will check with friends who may be interested in changing their eating and/or exercise habits. They may be able to help support each other and exercise together.

♦ If she has difficulty getting on track, she will meet with the college's health educator or nutritionist (to find out more, ask the RA or check the college website).

STEP-BY-STEP . . .
GREEK LIFE AND GREEK LIFE OFFICE: LEARNING THE ABCS (OR THE ALPHA BETA GAMMA) OF FRATERNITIES AND SORORITIES

Fraternities and sororities are social groups on campus that are also committed to community service and philanthropy. Some fraternities and sororities may be academic in nature. These organizations are considered part of "Greek Life," and often use Greek letters as their names. These organizations are usually, but not always, single-sex. Practices vary across different universities; for example, some Greek groups have houses or designated living spaces for members, whereas others do not. Costs for membership also vary.

There are many benefits of being a member of a sorority or a fraternity. These groups provide opportunities for students to build friendships and make connections with other students and alumni. These groups also find the community service and leadership opportunities valuable. Some students see Greek life as integral to their college experience.

On the other hand, there are concerns related to fraternities and sororities. The activities of Greek organizations often require a substantial time commitment, particularly during the initiation, or pledging, phase, which may last for several weeks or months. There have been instances of members participating in illegal and/or risky activities. Further, some groups have had problems with hazing, or initiation rituals that may be dangerous or humiliating, during the pledging process. It is important for each student who is considering joining a fraternity or sorority to fully consider the costs and the time commitment, as well as the possible benefits and risks.

For universities that have fraternities and sororities, the Greek life office is responsible for supporting these groups. The office helps fraternities and sororities with recruitment, educational programming, and compliance-related issues, and works to ensure that all members of the Greek system are benefiting from their experiences. The Greek Life office is a good resource for students considering joining a fraternity or sorority, and for current members of these groups as well.

STEP-BY-STEP . . .

FINANCIAL AID OFFICE: WHEN WHAT'S IN THE PIGGY BANK CAN'T COVER THE COST

All universities and colleges have a financial aid office. This is the department that determines financial need of the students and awards the financial aid. Most financial aid offices help students with all aspects of funding for college, including scholarships, loans, work-study jobs and grants. Because of the great amount of paperwork that goes into applying for financial aid, the financial aid office can also answer questions related to applications for aid and deadlines.

A university's financial aid office may also track students' grade point averages, since some scholarships are contingent upon students maintaining a minimum GPA. If a student is unsure about whether a scholarship awarded to them includes GPA requirements, it is important for the student to inquire with the financial aid office to find out. Sometimes a student's GPA may drop below the requirement for a scholarship. In these cases, the financial aid office may consider appeals from students.

The financial aid office works in conjunction with other offices on campus and provides additional support for students paying for their college education. They may provide a list of jobs on and off campus, and may work with the bursar's office/financial services office to provide billing information and payment plan options.

It is beneficial for students to have a good understanding of how to best contact the staff in their institution's financial aid office, whether it be by phone, email or in person, and to determine if there is one specific person assigned to them. The website for the financial aid office can also be very helpful in understanding deadlines as well as the different types of aid available.

CHAPTER 7

February

● ● ●

February 16
Dear Mom and Dad,

My life is not turning out exactly the way I was hoping for this semester. I took your advice and got involved with an activity that I "wouldn't normally do" and have been hangin' out with dudes and chicks I could never see myself with on any type of regular basis. This whole thing of rethinking who I spend time with has blown up in my face, and now my old squad thinks I am a total loser. Thanks a lot!

I know that you didn't want me to continue "associating myself" with Joe's crew since Cam got dismissed after first semester, but now I don't think joining the Student Activities Council was the answer to solving my problems. Joe wouldn't even come within ten feet of the first meeting. Anyways, our first project was Valentine-O-Grams. My job was to deliver the candies and messages to everyone whose "sweet hearts" bought one for them. I had to wear a PINK shirt while I was delivering these gay things, and I think, besides me, every other delivery boy WAS a fairy. To make matters worse, I am the ONLY guy on my floor who didn't get one of those stupid Valentine-O-Grams, so now everyone's definitely going to think I'M GAY.

My crew was already making fun of me for being a virgin, but I guess that's better than Joe's situation. He might have some kind of sexually transmitted disease and HIS "sweet heart" isn't talking to him and won't accept his Valentine-O-Gram, because she wasn't the one who gave give him the STD. He's been cryin' on my shoulders for days. I can't take all this stress, man. I can't believe I'm tellin' you guys all of this crap. Sometimes I just wish I was back at home and still with Kara.

Love,
Justin

Growing Pains: What May Be Breaking Your ~~Baby's~~ Young Adult's Heart This Month

* Facing challenges with intimate relationships
* Struggling with finding a "friend group" and fitting in
* Increasing concern over solidifying a comfortable social niche
* Dealing with the "winter blues"
* Experiencing a challenge to personal values
* Growing incidences of vandalism on campus resulting from frustration with "cabin fever"
* Mounting anxiety that mid-terms are approaching (depending on the structure and organization of the institution your young adult attends)

INTIMATE RELATIONSHIPS

I am beside myself. I got a disturbing text message from my son last night. The young men he hangs out with were teasing him relentlessly because he is still a virgin. He hasn't had a girlfriend since he went off to college, so he can't even lie to them to "save face." All through high school he had a nice girl for his companion, but we

discouraged him from entering into a serious relationship in college so he could focus on his studies. Have we made a mistake? What should we tell him?

When your child goes off to college, the ways in which he interacts with you and his peers will undergo significant changes. The good news is, he reached out to you to let you know what is going on in his world. Not to worry, you gave him sound advice. Indeed, college students should put their studies first. Still, in the adolescent stage of development, college students also have a growing desire to form intimate relationships. In fact, one psychologist, Erik Erikson, in his theory of psychosocial development, labels this desire as a stage in life called intimacy versus isolation. During this period, young adults experience a growing interest in forming intimate, loving relationships with other people. They feel a tension between feeling isolated and striving to cultivate relationships. Having said that, while your son's studies should come first, this time period in a young adult's life is also about learning what constitutes a healthy relationship. Perhaps your son would be capable of balancing a relationship and his school work. Further, it sounds like he had this type of companionship in high school and he may be missing that connection.

In addition to a growing desire to have companionship and to form intimate relationships, in the adolescent stage of development, teens and young adults may face a significant amount of peer pressure. For your son, it sounds like his values related to when it's appropriate to engage in sexual activity was challenged by his peer group. By reaching out to you, he opened the door to having a conversation with you. Take this opportunity to revisit your family's values around relationships, sex, and sexuality, keeping in mind that, during this stage of development, young adults often begin to explore how they are different from their parents in an effort to form their own identities. For instance, today's young adults may have more or less conservative views than you do related to sex, ranging from whether being in love should be a prerequisite for sex to the frequency of partners to what kinds of sexual behavior, such as oral sex, is acceptable.

What's important here is to talk to your son about reflecting on his values. If he chooses to maintain his virginity through the college years, he should be confident in his own decision. Further, if he is finding himself in uncomfortable situations, such as his friends "hazing" him about his virginity, he should work on asserting himself, and in the future, remove himself from these types of uncomfortable encounters. This situation represents an opportune time to talk to him about what it means to be a good friend. That is, would a good friend make fun of you for important choices you make? If the answer is no, then it may be time to think about finding a new crowd. The best advice to give him is, if the teasing is bothering him, he should evaluate whether he wants to continue being friends with the people who are teasing him. Certainly, if he determines that he doesn't want to continue with these friendships, he will identify other ways to build friendships with people who respect him and his values.

While it may seem overwhelming to dig into discussing these friendship choices with your son, the good news is that what your son is experiencing is common during the first-year of college and during the adolescent stage of development. Colleges and universities are aware of these typical issues and there are a wide variety of resources that he can access on his campus to help. You don't have to go at this alone with him. For instance, there are services on campus that can support him in creating the balance between his academic and social life, if this particular friend group is becoming all-consuming in an unhealthy way. Further, in terms of reflecting on whether these current friendships are healthy, services on his campus such as the **women's center** or **residence life office** are likely to offer educational programming like workshops or one-on-one support aimed at forming healthy relationships.

What to expect of your ~~baby~~ young adult in this situation:

- He will think about the crowd he is spending time with to determine whether the relationships he has formed are supporting his overall well-being or sabotaging his ability to be successful.
- He will examine services on campus that can support him in creating the balance between his academic and social life.

- He will examine the services on his campus to see what kinds of educational programming is offered.
- He will talk to someone he trusts, either campus resource personnel, you, or a good friend to address his comfort level with his virginity and sexual choices.

COMMUNITY MEMBERSHIP

My son called us last night very upset about a mandatory meeting in his residence hall. Some students broke into the president's house and stole a carpet with the university's insignia on it and placed it in the lobby of my son's dorm. Every student who lives in the hall was called to the meeting for questioning and asked if they knew ANYTHING about who might have done this. They were told to report what they knew to the campus police. Apparently, it's "guilty until proven innocent." My son had NOTHING to do with this. He thought it was extremely unfair that he had to take time out of studying because of the antics of some hoodlums. What should he do?

While it must be upsetting for you to feel like your son is receiving sanctions for "a crime that he didn't commit," and equally frustrating for your son to be pulled away from his studies, it is fairly common for resident directors to call hall meetings when institutional rules have been broken. Most colleges and universities operate under the philosophy that each student is a member of the larger community, and to a higher education community, that is taken very seriously. To educate students about community membership, most schools have some type of code of conduct or pledge.

A code of conduct typically focuses on the personal and intellectual growth of students. Intellectual conduct might address academic policies, such as rules about plagiarism; whereas, personal conduct normally encompasses behaviors outside of the classroom, which includes behaviors that take place in the residence halls. The beginning of one code of conduct reads, "It is a community with high standards and high expectations for those who choose to become a part of it, including established rules of conduct intended to foster behaviors that are consistent with a civil and educational setting" (Berkeley,_http://students.berkeley.edu/uga/conduct. pdf). Another institution describes their community similarly, "the campus is a place where high standards of civility are set and violations are challenged" (Bryant University Pledge, http://www.bryant.edu/student-life/housing/code-of-conduct.htm). Most institutions believe that joining their community is an honor, and being bestowed such an honor "requires each individual to uphold the policies, regulations, and guidelines established" (Hampton University, http://www.hamptonu.edu/about/codeof-conduct.cfm).

Given that colleges and universities dedicate a great deal of time to thinking about the climates they would like to create on their campuses and take their codes of conducts very seriously, it is likely your son's school, in this instance, decided to take this vandalism situation as an opportunity to educate the students about the community expectations. Oftentimes, institutions will carefully monitor the campus climate both inside and outside of the classroom and utilize the residence halls to "seize educational opportunities" beyond the confines of academics. There is a high probability that those who conducted the meeting know that your son didn't have anything to do with stealing the carpet; yet, in addition to investigating the vandalism to see if anyone knew or saw anything, they also took the opportunity to remind first-year students what the school's expectations are for them.

Try to discuss the university's perspective with your son. If you can encourage him to see the institution's point of view, chances are it will alleviate his feelings of being falsely accused of something he didn't do. Remind him that, in fact, he is a member of the community and has a shared responsibility to contribute to being a responsible member of it. He will always be a member of some type of community, whether it be the neighborhood in which he resides when he graduates or the community of professionals in his chosen career. Part of being in college is learning about responsible group membership.

What to expect of your ~~baby~~ young adult in this situation:

- He will familiarize himself with the institution's code of conduct or pledge.
- He will check back in with you to tell you what he has learned.
- He will discuss his feelings with the resident assistant or resident director.
- He will ask what the next steps are for the investigation into the vandalism and find out if there is anything he can do to help and/ or find out if there are any further expectations of him.

WINTER BLUES

I'm very concerned about my daughter. No matter what time I call her, it sounds like she's just woken up. The last few times I have spoken with her, she has just sounded so down and depressed. She even told me she has been missing classes on occasion because she has been sleeping in and having difficulty getting out of bed. This behavior is nothing like the energetic, motivated girl I know. I am hoping it's only the winter blues, but I don't know if I should be taking her behavior more seriously. We are from an area of the country where it's warm and sunny most of the year. She's just not used to the snow and cold.

For many students, the college adjustment period may take an entire academic year. If your daughter had a successful first semester, you may have assumed she would seamlessly transition into second semester. For some students, though, coming back for the second half of the year can be stressful; therefore, if you are concerned about behavior that is uncharacteristic of your daughter, then you should have a more in-depth conversation with her. On one hand, she may very well be experiencing a touch of the winter blues. If she ignores these feelings, the blues can hinder motivation and have a negative effect on grades. On the other hand, what she is experiencing may indicate that she is suffering from some type of depression.

Experiencing depression in college is not uncommon. Many college students are sleep deprived; they don't practice the healthiest eating habits, and they get stressed about keeping up on their schoolwork and managing their social relationships. As adults, we likely have established healthy coping mechanisms to deal with our stressors, such as exercising or reaching out to a friend for support. Unfortunately, the college environment can sometimes create depressive symptoms, particularly when students haven't yet established healthy ways of coping and they don't do a good job taking care of themselves.

During second semester, what used to seem exciting only a few months ago may now seem a little mundane and even boring. Add a lack of sleep, poor eating habits, and not enough exercise to the mix, and what started out as the winter blues may lead to low level or even more serious depression for some college students. Let's face it, we have all dealt with times when we are feeling a little down and would probably rather stay in bed on a rainy day or take a nap on a cold winter afternoon, but what's going on with your daughter could be more than just wanting to give into those feelings.

You may also want to consider the possibility that your daughter may be experiencing Seasonal Affective Disorder (SAD), a type of depression that's related to changes in seasons. Given that your family resides in a warmer climate, this could be a possibility. SAD begins and ends at about the same times every year. For most people with SAD, symptoms start in the fall and continue into the winter months. Symptoms include low energy, lethargy, and even moodiness. While there are effective ways to beat the winter blues such as establishing a daily routine, daily exercise, and even light therapy in order to boost energy, what seems to be important in this case is to determine exactly what is going on with her. Whether it's the winter blues, SAD, or depression, you need to get to the core of what's affecting her and creating behavior that is uncharacteristic of your daughter.

Fortunately, there are services on a college campus that can help your daughter address any of the mood shifts she may be experiencing whether it's the winter blues or more serious, like mild or moderate depression.

To address this concern, she may want to go to the institution's **counseling office** and investigate the services they have in place for depression screening. Staying active is also a key factor in warding off the winter blues. For instance, using the gym or getting involved in some activities would surely help. First steps here would be to look at the schedule of the gym and the offerings, such as exercise classes, or to inquire at the **student activities** or **involvement office** to see if there are any clubs or organizations she may be interested in. Talking with her **RA** or **residence hall director** about events and activities that will motivate her to get involved, and give her something to look forward to would also likely help. RA's are students who may have had the same experience; thus, they likely have some helpful advice to offer.

Routines are also important when addressing mood changes. Your daughter would likely feel the benefits of developing healthy eating, sleeping and exercise routines. One solution is to go to the academic support area to speak with an **advisor** or **learning specialist** about establishing a daily routine. Her RA may also be able to recommend other resources or advice.

There are a few other things you may want to ask her about. For instance, if she's skipped classes as a result of her depression, she should talk to her professor about the material she's missed. Friends can also be a support in these situations. They can provide social support. You may suggest that she reach out to a friend to do an activity with her, like going to the gym or catching a movie. Finally, if her boredom and lack of motivation do not decrease over the coming days she should visit counseling services or the **wellness center.**

What to expect of your ~~baby~~ young adult in this situation:

* She will seek out services at the institution that can help such as the counseling office or wellness center.
* She will make a concerted effort to try to stay active.
* She will go to the academic support area to speak with an advisor or learning specialist about establishing a daily routine including discussing developing healthy eating, sleeping and exercise routines.

- She will reach out to her RA or RD to see if they have any advice to offer.
- She will visit her professors during office hours to get back on track in the classes she has missed.
- She will reach out to friends for social support.

BIAS INCIDENT

My son is gay. He has been out since he was 15, and is a confident, happy young man. I was worried when he went away to college, because I was concerned that he might be subjected to homophobic behaviors by other students. Things seem to be going well, but he has mentioned that someone has been writing homophobic comments on the message board on his door. My son wants to just ignore it, but I am worried that this problem might escalate if he doesn't report it.

Sending your young adult to live away at college can be stressful for any parent. But when a parent is worried that their son or daughter may be bullied, harassed, is unsafe or unaccepted, the stress can be compounded. While it is reassuring that you and your son have open communication, it must be concerning to hear about an experience in which he has been subjected to homophobic comments.

It's understandable that you would like your son to report the comments so that they can be addressed. At the same time, at this stage in your son's life, he may not want to make waves with his new friends and the other people he is living with. If things are going well, he likely doesn't want to call attention to himself.

If he has a friend or two that he trusts, he should confide in them about his sexuality and about the comments written, if he hasn't already done so. By doing this, he is enlisting allies who can support him when he needs it.

Your son should also strongly consider telling his RA about the comments on his door. RAs are often the "eyes and ears" of the residence hall, and can make a point of checking your son's message board periodically, as well as being more mindful of any homophobic language being used in this living community.

It is likely that the RA may be obligated to report the message board incidents to the residence hall director. This professional staff member may ask your son some additional questions to get the full picture of the problem. From there, the residence hall director may determine that some actions need to be taken. These may include: offering educational programming on LGBTQ issues and/or appropriate residence hall community behavior; doing further investigation into who may have left these messages; and/or reporting these incidents to the **bias-related incident committee**. Depending on the campus's regulations, your son may have some say in which, if any, of these actions should be taken. However, because this is potentially a safety issue for your son, the RA and the residence hall director might have to document what happened. If your son is hesitant to take action, his first step could be consulting the student handbook to determine the specific protocols and policies at the institution.

Another possible resource for your son would be the campus's **LGBTQ center**. He could inquire about any confidentiality guidelines before discussing the incidents with professional staff there, if he is still hesitant to report the biased act through official channels. The LGBTQ center is also a resource that could provide your son with support. There is often a real sense of community formed around these centers, which can help him gain a better understand the campus climate related to issues around sexual orientation.

If your son decides not to disclose the incidents through official channels, he needs to be in communication with you and his allies about any similar homophobic incidents that arise. If you believe these incidents are escalating and your son is still unwilling to report the problem, this may be a time for you to step in. You should let your son know that you will take the step of calling the residence hall director to share what you know if he doesn't do so himself. And make that call.

What to expect of your ~~baby~~ young adult in this situation:

* He will enlist one or two friends on campus to be his allies.
* He will look into the confidentiality guidelines for reporting incidents to residence hall staff or to the LGBTQ center.

    *   He will disclose to his RA or the LGBTQ center if he determines that it is in his best interest to do so.

    *   If he determines that he doesn't want to report the prior incidents, he will communicate about any future incidents with you and his allies.

    *   If incidents escalate, he will report them to the appropriate channels, or you will.

BIAS RELATED BELIEF SYSTEMS

My daughter joined a new student group this semester in an effort to get more involved with activities on campus. She told us that a lot of lesbians are also in this group, and now she's being mistaken for one. I know she feels uneasy about this, but shouldn't she be more worried about her upcoming exams?

To start, of course your daughter should be worried about her upcoming exams, but the question she is raising here has more to do with another facet of adjusting to college besides academics. That is, figuring out where she fits in and questioning how she will be perceived based on with whom she decides to associate herself. Beyond the academic impact of going to college, to an extent, the college experience is influenced by exposure to people who are different from us.

Experiencing the diversity of a college campus can have a significant influence on a young person's worldview. The scope and nature of the influence will be affected by your daughter's openness and willingness to allow her new environment to inspire her to learn, change, and grow (Hazard & Nadeau, 2012). In fact, most college campuses pride themselves on creating diverse environments where students live and learn. Many college campuses carefully consider the rich experiences they intentionally create for students like a study abroad opportunity, for example. Regardless of race, ethnicity, gender, religion, sexual orientation, socioeconomic status, and age, institutions of higher education want to be seen as places that offer a welcoming community to ALL students.

In fact, scholars (Hyman and Jacobs, 2009) have researched the positive impact that experiencing a diverse environment can have on a young person's future. For example, diverse experiences can enhance self-awareness and promote creative thinking. Diversity also prepares students for future career success. Successful performance in today's diverse workforce requires sensitivity to human differences and the ability to relate to people from different cultural backgrounds. According to Hyman and Jacobs (2009), "America's workforce is more diverse than at any time in the nation's history, and the percentage of America's working-age population comprised of members of minority groups is expected to increase from 34 percent to 55 percent by 2050."

One result of colleges and universities understanding and recognizing the importance of diversity for their students' futures is a commitment to challenging and stopping acts of discrimination and hate on campuses. In other words, colleges and universities will challenge bias related belief systems. Indeed, colleges and universities have a variety of systems in place to assist in creating campus climates in which all students can thrive. In your daughter's case, she mentions concerns about participating in a club with lesbian students. On her campus, there is likely an LGBTQ Center (Lesbian, Gay, Bisexual, Transgendered and Questioning). Typically, these Centers have a goal to welcome LGBTQ students and their allies into the community and to diminish any type of prejudice that may limit the educational experiences and/or safety LGBTQ community members. Your daughter may want to utilize the **LGBTQ center** herself to gain a better understanding about social justice issues. For example, in institutions of higher education, the well-being of all members is supported, and in turn, students are expected to be supportive of each other regardless of race, ethnicity, gender, religion, sexual orientation, socioeconomic status, and age.

What to expect of your ~~baby~~ young adult in this situation:

- She will discuss questions or concerns she has about sexuality with a knowledgeable campus resource, such as a staff member from the LGBTQ center.
- She will explore the educational programming offered by the LGBTQ Center

- She will consider her reasons for joining the club/organization/ group in the first place, and if her reasons for joining are still valid and she values her membership, she will continue participating in this group.
- She will continue to balance her academic work with her co-curricular campus activities.

Peer And Cyber Peer Relationships

My son got involved with a cast of characters his first semester away at school. It sounds like all these young men did was party, play their video games, and scroll through Instagram. Needless to say, my son's GPA was not stellar. We suggested he find another group of friends who are more academically inclined and motivated, but he's having hard time finding his niche. What do you suggest?

Establishing connections with peers is increasingly done online today because so many students have easy access to popular sites that allow them to meet peers on the Internet. Many first-time college students welcome the opportunity to reinvent themselves, and the prospect of doing so in cyberspace is incredibly fun and appealing. Over the last few years though, there has been a steady growth in the percentage of people worldwide maintaining personal profiles on social networking sites, creating a situation where young people spend more and more time on social media outlets and gaming. Unfortunately, students' excessive time spent on the Internet and on their cell phones can be somewhat addictive and may contribute to potential problems. For instance, studies have shown that excessive time spent on the Internet increases the likelihood that students will lose sleep, be late to class, and have less direct communication with others, all factors that can add to to stress levels--something that college students definitely don't need (Hazard & Nadeau, 2012). Spending too much time gaming, like your son was doing, can certainly have negative effects.

What's important to determine in your son's case is to figure out whether he was spending time with "the gamers" because it was a way for him to fit in with peers or whether he was a willing participant, and spending time gaming was becoming addictive, thus detracting from his studies. In either case, he will want to put some strategies in place to refocus his energies toward his school work, and perhaps try using his time online or "gaming" as a reward after he completes his academic goals for the day. If he was spending time with this "cast of characters" in an effort to fit in and establish a peer group for himself, he may want to consider joining a club or organization that will fulfill the same "belonging" needs. His RA may have good club suggestions for him. That is not to say he can't maintain his friendships with the gamers, but perhaps he should just expand his horizons a bit.

While your son's situation is frustrating, the good news is that he did not experience any cyberbullying resulting from his excessive online use or gaming. Cyberbullying is when individuals use technology to bully others, which can cause extreme emotional distress. In cyberbullying situations, the experts advise to take down all social media profiles, avoid social media sites, and contact a university official immediately. For more information on cyberbullying, see http://cyberbullying.org/. Fortunately, your son's excessive time online did not escalate to cyberbullying, which can sometimes happen. Understandably, though, you are still worried about his time spent on the Internet. There are less extreme steps than taking down his profiles that your son can take to address the possible negative effect on his grades and to prevent the possibility of cyberbullying. For instance, a visit to a **learning specialist,** where he works on getting a handle on balancing his time spent on academic activities with the leisure time spent gaming could begin to get him on track.

What to expect of your ~~baby~~ young adult in this situation:

- He will meet with a learning specialist to work on some goal-setting and time management skills to create a balance between his leisure time and academic priorities.
- He will limit his gaming, cell phone use, and online time so that it does not interfere his studies.

- He will identify some interests he has beyond gaming and social media, and discuss with his RA ways to get involved with these interests on campus.
- He will consider joining a student organization or an academic club.

STEP-BY-STEP . . .
DEAN OF STUDENTS: INSURING YOUR ~~BABY~~ YOUNG ADULT IS PLAYING WELL WITH OTHERS

Colleges and universities have a dean's position dedicated to non-academic issues at the institution. This position is typically called the **dean of students**. The dean of students encourages student development and addresses student issues and needs, including planning and directing the university activities related to student services and campus life. Most also have the responsibility of handling discipline-related processes and procedures. Further, their role is to enforce an institution's **code of conduct** and to insure that students are following rules and regulations as outlined in a student handbook.

Colleges and universities have codes of conduct designed to ensure the safety and comfort of all members of the community. These codes typically outline the policies, procedures, rights, and responsibilities of students. A dean of students' office, for example, is usually responsible for enforcing these codes. If students violate their university's code of conduct, they are addressed through an official judicial process, which would likely be described in detail in the student handbook; therefore, it is critical that all first-years become familiar with the policies and procedures as outlined in their student handbooks.

STEP-BY-STEP . . .
LGBTQ CENTERS: FOSTERING A DIVERSE COMMUNITY FOR YOUR ~~BABY~~ YOUNG ADULT

Most colleges and universities have some type of department on campus with programs and services focused on supporting Lesbian, Gay,

Bi-Sexual, Transgendered, and Questioning (LGBTQ) students. Many colleges and universities further extend their programs and services to ALL members of their community, including faculty and staff. On some campuses, these departments are housed in an area called something like **the center for diversity and inclusion,** along with other similar campus resources like a **women's center.** On other campuses, an LGBTQ Center might be a stand-alone department called something like the LGBTQ Resource Center.

These departments are a safe space for LGBTQ students and their allies. While these types of centers provide a safe place for the LGBTQ community on campuses, they also typically provide resources for anyone who has questions about LGBTQ-related subjects or even issues of sexual and gender identity. These offices often provide educational programming on campuses and are designed to raise awareness of LGBTQ issues. These centers are committed to diversity and equity and work toward those goals through education, advocacy, and support. What is paramount for colleges and universities is to maximize the educational experience and safety of LGBTQ community members.

STEP-BY-STEP . . .
BIAS PREVENTION AND EDUCATION: ENCOURAGING YOUR ~~BABY~~ YOUNG ADULT TO TREAT EVERYONE EQUALLY

More broadly conceived than an LGBTQ Center or Women's Center, for example, many colleges and universities have moved to creating a model that encompasses addressing all dimensions of diversity including: race, religion, national origin, ethnicity, sexual orientation, disability, and gender status. On many campuses now, you will see a place called a Center for Diversity and Inclusion (CDI). Basically, the goal of these centers is to provide programs, services, education, support, and advocacy with the sole purpose of increasing members of an institution's appreciation of and sensitivity to issues related to diversity. Some of these centers take the approach where they help students engage in cross-cultural exploration, for example, to help them develop a deeper understanding of their own individual identity, in order to more deeply understand others' identities. Some of these centers may design programs and services aimed at supporting racially and ethnically underrepresented students. Ultimately, these centers focus on continually enhancing an institution's commitment to diversity and inclusion. A center for diversity and inclusion is also deeply concerned with acts of discrimination and hate that might occur on a college campus as well.

Indeed, most colleges and universities are committed to challenging and stopping acts of discrimination and hate. Toward this end, many schools have some type of **bias-related incident committee**, which are put in place to monitor and investigate the occurrence of bias incidents on college campuses. These committees investigate incidents and make recommendations for educational programs and standards of action. Typically, a student handbook would provide information about reporting procedures if a student were to experience a bias incident.

Students should understand the distinction between a bias incident and a hate crime. A bias incident is a threatened, attempted, or completed action that is motivated by bigotry and bias regarding a person's real or perceived race, religion, national origin, ethnicity, sexual orientation, disability, or gender status. Examples of these incidents include name calling, offensive language/acts, graffiti, or inappropriate gestures/behavior. A hate crime is a criminal act, including physical assault or vandalism, in which the victim is a target because of their real or perceived race, religion, national origin, ethnicity, sexual orientation, disability, or gender. What's most important is that students understand there are resources and services on campus to help them navigate the diverse climate of an institution of higher education. The key for your college student is to familiarize themselves with the campus resources designed to address their concerns and to feel comfortable accessing them.

CHAPTER 8

March

● ● ●

March 17th

Dear Dad and Mom,

Happy St. Patrick's Day‼! Who woulda thought that I'd be celebrating St. Patrick's Day in Mexico?!

It's definitely crazy here, but I'm OK. Henry and Dan are out of control though. Believe it or not, I'm the sane one out of all my friends here. We have been drinking lots of beer, but I've also had some new exotic drinks that I never tried before.

You know those girls who live down the hall, Kelly and Christina? They're here, too. Kelly was kind of freaked out when I saw her this morning. I guess Christina was out all night, and just came back to the hotel in tears. I don't know what happened, but it can't be good.

I know this Spring Break trip definitely is worth it, but I am starting to wonder how I'm going to pay my bills when I get back. I'm putting everything on my new credit card, and I don't really understand the conversion stuff with pesos and dollars. Hopefully, I'm not spending too much dinero.

If I don't call you right when I get back to campus, don't worry. It's just that I have a lot of work to do, including a 25 page research paper that I haven't even started yet.

Adios!
Elliot

Growing Pains: What May Be Keeping Your ~~Baby~~ Young Adult Awake This Month

* Coming up with money for spring break
* Experiencing excitement and/or nervousness about traveling without family for the first time
* Feeling bummed out about spending time at home while other students may be vacationing
* Struggling with poor behavior choices related to alcohol use
* Worrying about isolation from friends because of diverging values
* Mounting credit-card debt from spring break escapades
* Stressing over end-of-term projects, papers and exams

Unhappy Homecoming

My daughter is coming home next week for spring break. While I was expecting that she'd like to go away with some of her college friends, she said she'd rather come home and relax. But now she seems to be really negative about missing out on a good time. I think her attitude may have to do with the fact that none of her high school friends have the same week off after all. I hope she's not miserable the whole time she's home.

It sounds like your daughter regrets her decision to skip spring break with her friends. How about talking to her to find out the reasons she originally did not want to go away with them? There are likely many explanations for why she made her original plans to come home. Perhaps she was being frugal with her finances, and didn't want to take a trip that would cost too much money. Maybe she was hoping to see an old boyfriend from high school that she expected to be home. Or, she may have felt uncomfortable with the kinds of plans her friends made for the trip.

Whatever the reason, she needs to come to grips with her decision, whether or not she now feels like it was the right one. If she was concerned, for example, about the drinking and partying she expected her friends to partake in, then you can help her recognize that she made a responsible choice to come home, and that her decision is aligned with her values. After all, some spring break destinations have reputations for wild activities, such as wet t-shirt contests, hooking up, beer pong, and pole dancing parties. On the other hand, if she had missed out on the trip in hopes of seeing her old boyfriend, she may now regret it and need to work through what she feels like was a bad choice.

For college students, one of the worst feelings is coming back to campus after spring break and hearing all the "crazy stories" about the fun they may have missed. At the moment, she is probably witnessing all the excitement and anticipation about the upcoming trip from her friends, so she is likely second guessing her initial decision.

Once she is home, you can encourage her to make good use of her time. Often students are feeling fatigued from the rigors of the first half of the semester and some quality naptime at home can help recharge them for the rest of the semester. If your daughter has any projects or exams upon her return to campus, she may find that the relative quiet of home is a good place to get ahead academically.

What to expect of your ~~baby~~ young adult in this situation:

* She will think through her reasons for deciding to stay home instead of traveling for spring break.
* She will take advantage of her time at home to rest and rejuvenate herself.
* She will use this time to look at the work she has left for the remainder of the semester, and see if she can get ahead a bit, so she feels less stressed when finals roll around.

TRAVELING CONCERNS

My son has made plans to go away on "alternative spring break" with some other members of his fraternity. They are going to New Orleans to work on restoring some houses. He has never even been on an airplane before, and I don't think he is savvy enough yet to travel without me and his mother. While I am really proud of him for doing this, I am not feeling comfortable with him going away without a real adult.

Alternative spring break is a movement among college and high school students to use their time away from school to do good work instead of simply vacationing. This is a great opportunity for young adults to do community service, while learning about themselves and the world around them. Working on restoring houses in New Orleans will give your son the chance to find out more about an important event in U.S. history (Hurricane Katrina), to experience life in a different city, and to bond with his fraternity brothers.

That said, traveling without a parent or other "grown-up," while a milestone of young adulthood, can be anxiety-producing for parents and for their young adult as well. It will feel like the first time he left you to go to preschool or to a sleepover. All day and night, you may find yourself thinking, I hope he's OK; I wonder what he's doing now. It's a whole new stressful time of having to let go a bit so that your son can further develop self-sufficiency and independence.

If you haven't done so already, speak with your son regarding his feelings about the trip, and try to determine whether he feels comfortable traveling with peers. This will allow him the opportunity to ask you questions about the experience, and will give you the chance to better assess his readiness.

You can share some travel tips and strategies with your son, including:

* Having contact information for the trip's planner, whether that is a travel agent, or the fraternity member who is organizing the trip
* Printing out a trip itinerary, including details on where he will be staying and visiting
* Checking with the airline about what can be brought on a plane, including carry-on guidelines

* Checking with the airline about flight details, and understanding what happens during layovers and transfers
* Bringing his driver's license or other photo identification
* Staying with other people he knows when traveling around the city
* Bringing an appropriate amount of cash with him for the trip, and during daily travels
* Storing his valuables safely in the hotel or place he is staying, or leaving unneeded valuables at home entirely
* Keeping his room locked at all times

If your son does the research and preparation himself on these issues, he will feel more independent and well-prepared to travel without you. Once he's done this work, you may also feel more comfortable with him going on this trip.

You may also feel less nervous if you have more information and details on the trip. Request that your son provide you with the flight numbers, the itinerary, and the address of where he will be staying in New Orleans. If possible, get an alternative telephone number, whether it's a fraternity brother's cell phone or the hotel where he is staying, in case you need to reach him and his cell phone isn't functioning. Before he leaves, make an agreement with your son about how often he should be in contact with you while he is away.

What to expect of your ~~baby~~ young adult in this situation:

* He will research all the details of his trip using the checklist.
* He will share this research with you.
* He will stay with other people in his party at all times.
* He will keep contact with you in accordance with your prearranged agreement.

RESEARCH PAPER WOES
My daughter is panicking. She returned to campus after more than a week off, and now she is overwhelmed by the amount of school work

she still needs to complete before the end of the semester. For her 20 page history research paper, she was supposed to submit all of her sources to her professor, but she hasn't even chosen her topic yet. She was home all last week, and never cracked a book! Is it too late for her to tackle such a huge project?

When academic projects seem too big or overwhelming, first year students sometimes try to forget about them in hopes that they will go away. They won't.

Your daughter is behind schedule, but she can still succeed with this project. The first thing she should do is go speak with her professor. She should be honest about her situation, and find out if the professor would be willing to accept the sources late. Recall the advice from September about ways in which to approach professors. Remind her that when she meets with her professor, she should take total responsibility for her procrastination in this situation.

Once she has put out the fire of this overdue portion of the assignment, she can then turn her attention to the work ahead of her. A research paper is a project with many facets and requirements. Your daughter should make a list of all the smaller tasks, the baby steps that the project involves, and set some due dates for herself, working toward the official date on which she needs to turn in the paper. By listing these intermediate steps for the project as due dates in her calendar or planner, your daughter may feel more in control and less overwhelmed.

Fortunately, there are also resources available to help your daughter with this project. In addition to discussing the project and some of her topic ideas with her professor, your daughter would do well to seek out help from the college's writing center. There, she can get some guidance on choosing a topic, planning her steps, developing a working thesis, and finding a system to cite all of her sources. She will likely need to visit her professor and the writing center more than one time, as she moves forward with her paper.

Your daughter should also get to her **campus library** as soon as possible. The reference librarians can help her with all parts of her research. She will need to do some preliminary research in order to choose an appropriate topic. From there, she will likely need to refer to several types of sources, possibly including primary sources, peer-reviewed journals, and books. The librarians can assist her in finding these materials. See the Step-By-Step later in this chapter for more information on the excellent services of many college libraries.

This project will be a challenge for your daughter, and she has lots of long hours and difficult work ahead of her. She may need encouragement to continue working through to the end of it. If she doesn't think she can complete it in time, she should talk with her professor as soon as possible.

What to expect of your ~~baby~~ young adult in this situation:

- She will visit her professor immediately to discuss the work she has missed and arrange a way to make it up, if possible.
- She will discuss the paper with her professor, and make sure she has a clear understanding of the assignment.
- She will break the components of the project into smaller pieces and record due dates for herself in her calendar for each component leading up to the final due date.
- She will meet with someone in the writing center to discuss questions and concerns she has with the project and to review her writing as it progresses.
- She will go to the library and work with a reference librarian to find appropriate, useful sources for her paper.
- If she continues to struggle with this project, she will discuss her problems with her professor.

RECKLESS BEHAVIOR AND SOCIAL MEDIA

I have been looking at some of my son's pictures from spring break on social media. I can't believe some of the inappropriate things he and his friends are doing in these photos! I am disappointed in him, and concerned about his reckless behavior, not to mention the fact that he posted these shots on online for all to see.

Remember when your son would have been mortified if you had shown his friends his baby pictures? Apparently, those days are over! To this generation, there is nothing really off-limits, nothing not worthy of sharing with other "friends" on social media.

Although the use of social media is such an integral part of many college students' lives, they don't necessarily critically or reflectively consider the appropriateness of their posts, whether those are status updates, photos, links or videos. Your son seems not to have filtered out any material as unsuitable for sharing with the world.

Many young adults don't realize how much their social media usage shapes the way that others perceive them. Their online profiles may tell the world about them, but don't necessarily present them accurately. But whether or not the profile is an accurate portrayal, it is still available for everyone to see. These profiles can be accessed by potential internship programs and employers. They are seen by other students and members of the university community. And they are even available to parents, aunts and uncles, and grandparents.

It would be beneficial to have a serious discussion with your son about the impressions his pictures and posts may be giving others. For example, there may be photos of him "partying." Perhaps he did indeed party on his spring break vacation, but when he is at school, he does take care of his responsibilities and keeps his "partying" to a minimum. Posts like this can give the impression that he's a "party animal" and engages in this behavior consistently. Is that the image he wants to project to the outside world?

Another factor your son needs to consider is that if he is posting photos of his friends in compromising positions, he may create negative impressions of them as well. What if one of his friends misses out on an internship opportunity because the person doing the hiring saw a picture of him doing shots of alcohol with your son? Your son's social media profile is not only a reflection on him, but also on anyone he associates with. You bringing this to his attention may have an even stronger effect on him than discussing his own self-portrayal, and may lead to his removing these photos.

The second issue with your son and his spring break posting is that you are seeing evidence of behaviors that are clearly opposed to those that you have come to expect of your son. For instance, if you have always stressed the importance of showing respect to women, and you see a photo of him as an enthusiastic spectator at a wet t-shirt contest, it can be very disheartening to see that he isn't practicing the values you taught him. Next time you have an opportunity for a face-to-face extended conversation, discuss with your son the conflicts you have observed between his values and his actions.

You may want to consider, and discuss with your son, other possible negative consequences or repercussions of his behaviors. For example, if you paid for his spring break trip, would his behaviors during this recent vacation cause you to reconsider financing future travels? Or, what would happen if a prospective employer saw these photos?

What to expect of your ~~baby~~ young adult in this situation:

- He will remove any online photos that show him or his friends in compromising positions.
- He will learn more about how social media can be viewed by friends, family, acquaintances and strangers.
- He will discuss with you the events of Spring Break and how they may or may not correspond with his values.

Sexual Assault

My daughter just called me after returning to campus from home. She says that her roommate, who went to Florida with some friends during spring break, was raped while on vacation. Her roommate hasn't told anyone else about this; both she and my daughter are extremely emotional right now. What do I do from here?

What you *have* to do is get help for both of them immediately, particularly for your daughter's roommate, the survivor of the sexual assault. Without a doubt, this is a time to call in the experts. If your daughter and her roommate are at a college close by, you may want to call a rape crisis hotline in your community to get some initial advice on how to handle the situation. If they are living away at school, and it is too far away for you to get there in person, almost ALL colleges and universities have rape crisis services on campus either as a stand-alone service, through the college or university **counseling center**, or in a **women's center**. In the immediate aftermath of a rape, getting safety and support measures in place is critical for the subsequent recovery after this traumatic event, as is working with family and close friends (like your daughter) of the victim.

Indeed, rape is a trauma with physical, emotional, and behavioral side effects. Victims often react with symptoms of depression, such as experiencing nightmares, an inability to sleep, feelings of nausea, becoming silent and withdrawn, and being prone to intermittent bouts of crying. What is also typical are feelings of guilt, fear, and embarrassment. Most of all, survivors feel that somehow the rape was their fault; they feel like they will be blamed if others find out. It is imperative for survivors to be assured that the assault was NOT their fault.

Rape crisis experts identify three phases survivors encounter. In phase one, the victim is in extreme stress or shock. There is not necessarily a single reaction; it's highly individualized and connected to the person's typical ways of coping with stressful life events. In phase two, the victim may appear like they have accepted what's happened to them and the prevailing attitude of "I am just going to have to live with this" emerges. The idea of putting the incident behind seems appealing; though it is likely that there will be remaining debilitating symptoms. In phase three, victims begin to think more and more about what happened, symptoms may return and the "forgetting about it" strategy functions less and less.

Whatever symptoms your daughter's roommate is experiencing and whatever phase of survival she is in, you *must* mobilize support for them. Contrary to the majority of advice offered in this book, this is certainly the time for you to hover, interfere, take control, and get appropriate assistance. No matter what the age, a victim of sexual assault needs expert help, advice, guidance, and assistance. Right now, you need to access advice from the experts and do exactly what they tell you to do to support your daughter and her roommate. Rely on community and campus experts.

What to expect of your ~~baby~~ young adult in this situation:

* She will defer to your advice and that of campus experts on sexual assault.

* She will give unyielding support to her roommate.
* She will seek emotional support for herself if she needs it.

CREDIT CARD DEBT

I just checked my daughter's credit card bill online. She is maxed out, and it looks like she spent up to her credit limit on flip-flops, swimsuits, and some pricey meals during her spring trip to visit her friend at another college. I am irritated with her for getting into debt over such trivial purchases.

Your daughter may be a novice with a credit card, and may not fully understand that her spending spree is going to have larger repercussions than the short-lived trip to visit her friend. If this is the case, she needs to learn more about how credit cards work. She should find out more about her interest rate, what her minimum payment is, when payments are due, and how long it will take for her to pay off her purchases. She can find this information by reviewing her next bill, by calling the credit card company or by visiting its website.

It may also be helpful for her to get a better understanding of what credit scores mean, and how they are earned. Your daughter, like many others her age, is probably not thinking about her credit score and how it may impact her in the future. She may be surprised to learn that potential employers, landlords, and other lenders will use her credit score to determine whether or not she is an appropriate person to hire, rent to or lend money to. This may be a shocking, but necessary, awakening for your daughter. You can share this information with her or recommend she research credit scores herself.

Another issue for you and your daughter to address is how to pay this bill. Depending on your family's values and ideas about money, you will have to decide whether or not you are willing to pay this bill for her. If you aren't handling this expense for her, how will it get paid off? Does your daughter have a job? If so, what can she pay toward the balance? If not, is it appropriate for her to find one now, or during the upcoming summer?

Regardless of how the bill is going to be paid, you need to find the opportunity to speak to your daughter about money, values and expectations. You can discuss her approach toward money during this trip, and how it differs or lines up with her other money practices. Is this totally out of character for your daughter, or is this a habit seen in other areas of her purchasing as well? If so, the two of you can work together to establish guidelines and rules for handling finances going forward.

What to expect of your ~~baby~~ young adult in this situation:

* She will contact her credit card company to determine her interest rate and payments.
* She will learn about credit scores so that she can make more informed decisions in the future.
* She will pay her credit card bill in accordance with the approach you agree upon with her, whether that is through a loan or gift, her existing job, or her soon-to-be acquired job.
* She will discuss her finances with you, and work with you to establish financial guidelines and rules for future purchases.

Step-By-Step . . .

The Library: Beyond the ABCs of Board Books

Libraries at colleges and universities are vital resources for today's college students. Most have moved far past the dusty shelves, card catalogs, and shushing staff to become an interactive, high-tech hub of academic work. Successful students often find that the libraries on their campuses have lots to offer to help them succeed in their courses.

First, the libraries at many colleges are excellent places to study. Most provide quiet spots to work in comfortable chairs and desks. Students who find their dorm rooms too distracting to get work done (and they *are* that distracting) often welcome the limited distractions of the library. Many libraries also provide study areas or rooms for group meetings, so that classmates can get together to prepare for exams or develop class presentations. The hours of operation for campus libraries are aligned with the college student's schedule, with late hours and even some 24 hour availability during final exams or other key times of the academic year. College libraries today often allow food and drink in some or all areas, so that students can work for extended periods of time if they need to, without having to leave the facility. It's not uncommon to even find cafes and vending machines in the library.

Of course, the library's central role on campus is to support the research done by the university's students and faculty. But most have moved beyond simply the books and microfiche of days gone by. The information and resources available are far more sophisticated, in keeping with today's technology. Libraries' card catalogs are now accessed via computer, as are the majority of their journal, newspaper and magazine articles. In fact, students can often search these resources via computer from anywhere, on or off campus.

Because so much more information is now available to the student researcher, the project of doing academic research can be daunting, especially for first year students. The **reference librarians** at campus libraries are on hand to support and educate students on how to do research, beyond simply Googling their topic or going to Wikipedia. They can help guide students to the best materials for their area of study, and to sources that professors would accept as reliable.

Many libraries provide other services, as well. Professors may put required or recommended course materials on reserve for students to check out, read or watch. They also typically have computers, printers, and scanners for students to utilize (most charge a fee for printing). Students can find out all of their library's offerings by visiting the library. Many offer tours to students. Students can also gain a great deal of information about the library by visiting its website.

Step-By-Step . . .

The Women's Center: Where Girl Power is Not Just for Women

The number of female students on college campuses is on the rise. According to the National Center for Education Statistics (http://nces.

ed.gov/pubs2005/equity/Section8), the proportion of the undergraduates who are female increased from the minority to the majority of students between 1970 and 2000; in 1970, 42 percent of all undergraduates were female, while in 2000, 56 percent were female. As a result, institutions of higher education offer resources and support to the increasing number of women students on campuses nationwide.

These programs and services are designed to educate campus communities about a wide variety of issues affecting women and men. While these services are often housed in a place called a women's center, the educational programming that is offered can certainly benefit everyone on campus, and the nature and scope of what is offered varies among campuses. The centers range from simply providing a safe, nonsexist environment in which students can study and relax while on campus, to offering counseling to providing rape crisis intervention.

The most common services typically include free resources and referrals regarding women's health, body image information, eating disorders, sexuality, and other gender-related issues faced by students. A goal of many women's centers is to raise awareness about sexism and its consequences, and to work toward ending violence, abuse, and all forms of sexist oppression. For example, it would not be unusual to see a women's center organizing various educational and consciousness-raising events, such as a "Take Back The Night" March (http://www.takebackthenight.org/) or a Breast Cancer Awareness Walk (http://ww5.komen.org/).

Students can find out more about whether their campus has a women's center or similar services by checking with their RA, or by looking at the college's website.

STEP-BY-STEP . . .
RAPE CRISIS SERVICES: FACING AN UNSPEAKABLE NIGHTMARE
According to the Rape, Abuse, and Incest National Network (http://www.rainn.org), 1 in 6 women, and 1 in 33 men, will be sexually assaulted in their lifetime. While this is extremely disturbing, college age women are four times more likely to be victims of sexual assault than their non-college

counterparts. Nearly ALL college campuses have comprehensive support services for individuals of all gender expressions who are survivors of sexual assault, intimate partner or domestic violence, childhood sexual abuse, or sexual harassment. Besides individual counseling and support groups for survivors, services may include legal and medical advocacy, and counseling for significant others. Although the rape crisis interventions may vary, most provide some type of an on-call support network for both female and male students.

Campus personnel who staff such networks have received training in rape crisis intervention, counseling, and support. They are available to help students understand the options they face in the event of a sexual assault and they will remain with the student throughout the entire process of addressing and/or adjudicating an incident.

Students can be assured that their phone calls will be confidential. Most often, students can choose to speak either with a male or female staff member. This person will assist them through the decision making process of going to the hospital and/or the police. The person will be their advocate in explaining campus sexual assault policies and procedures, and will offer support to the student through the entire process

CHAPTER 9

April

● ● ●

Dear Dad:

Hooray for spring! It's finally starting to warm up here on campus. It was 70 degrees yesterday, so we all skipped class and went sunbathing this afternoon. I don't want to lose my tan from spring break!

This weekend is spring weekend, so there are tons of parties planned. The next weekend is the Spring Fling, which I've been helping to plan. It's a lot of work, but I want to be the chair of the Spring Fling committee next year, so I am trying hard to help as much as I can. It's almost easy to forget about school work with all the other fun stuff going on right now.

While I have my dress for the Spring Fling picked out, I'm still not exactly sure who I'm going with. I was waiting for Sam to ask me, but I can't wait around forever, so I might ask Alex to be my date, or just go with a bunch of the other girls on my floor. I really like Sam, and would love if we could hook up this summer, since our hometowns are so close to each other!

I know you are wondering about how my classes are going. I should have this whole school thing down by now, but I'm still falling behind on all the stuff I have due. I don't have as much interest in my psychology class as I thought

I would, so I am not sure if that should be my major after all. That's kind of stressing me out, too.

See you next month!
MiKayla

Growing Pains: What May Be Giving Your ~~Baby~~ Young Adult Spring Fever This Month

* Feeling academic pressures as the semester nears an end, with papers, projects and exams due
* Increasing concern with weight loss and physical appearance due to warmer weather
* Experiencing a sense of spring fever, with bursts of energy for some and decreased focus on academics for others
* Focusing on romantic relationships, due to formal events like spring galas on the horizon
* Experiencing stress related to declaring or changing a major
* Realizing that there are new opportunities opening up at school as they transition to sophomore year

ACADEMIC PRESSURES

This entire school year, my son has been adjusting to college-level coursework. I thought by now, he would have his academics down pat. However, when we just spoke, I got the sense that he has several impending assignments and exams before the semester ends. He is stressed out and I'm worried for him. He really wants to get a good GPA, so he can apply for the major he is interested in.

For some students, the transition to college level academics can take longer than just one semester. Your son sounds like he is still in the midst of this transition.

Each semester and each course comes with its own unique challenges. Despite having made some progress with his coursework, this could be the first time he has been faced with so many assignments and exams in a compressed time frame. He will likely need to take some action very soon to ensure he is on track to have a strong finish to his semester.

The first thing your son needs to do is reach out to academic resources. He should visit his professors during their **office hours** and make sure he fully understands the final requirements in his classes. From there, he should determine whether he needs to meet with tutors, form study groups, visit the **writing center** and/or make additional visits to office hours. If he is struggling with planning his time for completing all of his projects, he should meet with a **learning specialist**, who can help with creating to-do lists and schedules for the final weeks of the semester. It would also be helpful for your son to speak with his **academic advisor** to further discuss the GPA requirements for his major and to calculate what final grades he will need in his classes to meet that requirement. The professional staff in the academic support areas are accustomed to helping students who may have waited until the last minute, and will gladly assist him.

If you also have the sense that your son is worried or stressed out, he may need to find some productive outlets for his stress. Perhaps he finds time at the gym to be a stress reducer. He should continue using healthy approaches to stress so that he has the energy and the mindset to study for his exams and to finish his projects. If he finds that his stress level is negatively impacting his ability to get his work done, he may want to consider speaking someone in **counseling services**.

What to expect of your ~~baby~~ young adult in this situation:

* He will reach out to academic resources, including tutors, professors, and learning specialists to help finish the semester strongly.
* He will talk to his academic advisor about GPA requirements for his intended major.
* He will find ways to relieve stress in a healthy way.
* He will talk with someone in counseling services if his stress level is negatively impacting him.

Spring Fever

Talking to my daughter, you'd never guess that school was in session. Her life seems to revolve around a variety of spring events going on at her college. She has become quite involved in clubs this year, which is great. But each club seems to be having some sort of spring fling event, and she's at the center of planning each of them. How is she supposed to maintain her GPA?

It sounds like your daughter is having a great time at college, but it's understandable that you are concerned. After all, you want her to be able to return in the fall, right?

It may be a good time to have a conversation with your daughter about your concerns. During that conversation, you may find that she has her course work under control, along with her extracurricular activities. If you get the sense that she is prioritizing her school work and that she is using good time management strategies for organizing her commitments, she is likely on the right track.

If, however, you feel that she is having difficulty managing her time, you may want to recommend that she meet with a **learning specialist** to look at how to better balance her academics with her social commitments. The learning specialist (See Step-By-Step in October) can help your daughter identify the time she needs to complete key tasks, reflect on what behaviors are effective and ineffective in managing her commitments, and identify areas that she may want to improve. For instance, she may have to delegate some of the event planning she has taken on to other club members.

If it proves to be the case that your daughter's academics have in fact suffered this semester, it will be important for her to talk to her professors as soon as possible to find out whether she can improve in their classes. Her **academic advisor** can also present her with options related to maintaining her GPA.

What to expect of your ~~baby~~ young adult in this situation:

- She will prioritize her school work over other activities.
- She will use a planner or other means to organize her time and her commitments, both academic and social.

- She will talk with a learning specialist should she have difficulty managing her time.
- If she is having difficulty maintaining her grades, she will speak to her professors and her academic advisor.

Spring Romance

The students in my son's residence hall seem to be living a full-fledged soap opera. I don't know how they keep track of who is going out, hanging out, hooking up, etc. The latest drama is centered on the spring formal. It sounds like two young ladies are both interested in going with him, and my son isn't sure what to do. I thought this was high school stuff!

While some of the behaviors you are hearing about from your son sound like "high school," they are often inevitable when there are adolescents living together in close quarters. Residence hall living can create plenty of opportunities for romantic drama. The good thing is that you don't have to worry about keeping track of all this drama! In your conversations with your son, you can help him process what he's experiencing, though.

Your son needs to seriously consider the impact of the goings-on in his residence hall. Are they causing him excess stress? Is he concerned about his courses and ability to get his work done? Has there been an impact on his friendships? If the atmosphere in his residence hall is negatively impacting him, you can encourage him to look for ways to extricate himself a bit. Perhaps getting off campus for a weekend would help. Or maybe he could refocus on his academics and spend more time studying in the library.

It would be most beneficial for your son to talk to a peer he trusts about what's going on and about his romantic relationships. He could talk to a friend, either on campus or a friend from home, his roommate, or even his **RA.** They may be able to provide him with some good, objective feedback on what's going on, and share their perspective on what they observe.

What to expect of your ~~baby~~ young adult in this situation:

* He will make academics his priority during the final weeks of his semester.
* He will seriously consider whether the dramatics of his residence hall are negatively impacting him in any way. If they are, he will look for ways to pull back from the drama.
* He will talk with someone he trusts, such as a friend, roommate or RA, if he needs feedback about his romantic relationships.

CHOOSING A MAJOR

My daughter is having a meltdown about her major. She chose her college based on its excellent pre-med program, but after a full year of science classes, she is having serious doubts about becoming a physician. It's OK with us if she changes her major, but she is at a total loss about her career choice.

It's really common for college students to change their minds about their majors. In fact, many universities and colleges are encouraging students to wait to declare a major until they've had some opportunities to explore several fields through their coursework and co-curricular activities. Fortunately, because this questioning of major or field of study comes up frequently among college students, there are many resources for your daughter to utilize as she makes decisions related to her major.

First, your daughter should talk with people who are involved in the pre-med program at her college, both professors and students. She can ask them questions about the future courses and the types of learning she can expect in the coming semesters. For example, she may find that the first-year pre-med course work is particularly onerous, but gets more manageable during sophomore year.

Your daughter also has an **academic advisor,** who she should meet with to discuss her concerns about her major. The advisor can provide her with options for changing majors within the university and help her understand how her pre-med credits can be applied if she decides to pursue a different degree, either at her current university or at a different one. The advisor can also answer any questions about deadlines related to making a decision about her major. For example, if your daughter decides she wants to wait one more semester before making a final decision about changing majors, will that have any consequences?

The university's **career services office** is another excellent resource for your daughter. The staff in career services can help your daughter explore her interests and strengths, and the careers connected to them. She may be able to attend a career exploration workshop that will help her find a direction she is more comfortable with; alternatively, she may find that there is a career path for the pre-med major that she hadn't yet considered.

Once your daughter has all of the information she needs, she can make an informed decision with you.

What to expect of your ~~baby~~ young adult in this situation:

- She will talk with professors and/or other students in her current major to address concerns she may have about her field of study.
- She will meet with her academic advisor to talk about her options for her major.
- She will visit the career services office to find out how they can help her explore majors and careers that may interest her.
- She will discuss this issue with you and involve you in the decision making process.

Concerns About Appearance

Ever since I shipped my son a box of his spring clothes, he has been complaining about his weight. Apparently, none of his clothes fit him anymore, and I think he is embarrassed about having put on some weight during the winter months at school. At the same time, it sounds like his only extracurricular activity is playing video games with his roommate. Is there anything he can do on campus to get more fit, or should he just wait until he gets home for the summer?

The winter months can be difficult for many of us in terms of staying active. As your son found out, staying indoors and playing video games can be a good way to socialize when the weather isn't cooperating, but extended periods of sitting in one place can lead to weight gain. The fact that he is complaining about his weight seems to indicate that your son may be ready to make a change to his habits.

Fortunately, many college campuses have plenty of resources and opportunities for students to get active. There are often fitness centers, sports fields and campus clubs that allow students to participate in whatever forms of exercise they like. You may be able to help your son brainstorm some physical activities that he would enjoy based on his interests. For example, if your son always found soccer a great pastime, he may want to look into whether there is an **intramural** soccer league. Or, if he enjoys running, he may want to visit the track or the gym's treadmills. He may need a just a little encouragement to change his mind-set about how he is spending his free time.

While his recent sedentary behavior is likely impacting his weight gain, your son may also find that he has developed some different eating habits over the winter months as well. For many people, a combination of these two factors impacts their weight. The university's nutritionist or **wellness center** staff member can help your son get back on track with what he eats and can advise him on how much exercise would be most beneficial to him.

If your son is resistant to changing his physical activity or eating habits while away at college, or is having difficulty doing so, it would be advisable to continue this conversation when he is home for the summer. He may find that being home will allow him to re-instill more positive habits. His doctor or other health professional who knows him well could provide valuable advice in this area.

What to expect of your ~~baby~~ young adult in this situation:

- He will consider what kind of exercise he likes to do, and find ways to regularly incorporate it into his schedule.
- He will look into the exercise programs, including gym access, intramural sports, and clubs that the university offers.

♦ He will meet with a nutritionist or other member of the wellness center staff to discuss his eating and other health habits.

New Opportunities

My daughter is so excited. She has been talking to some of the upper class students who live in her residence hall, and they have been telling her about all sorts of new programs and opportunities she can take advantage of once she is no longer a freshman. She sounds like a kid in a candy shop, talking about internships, studying abroad, joining a sorority, becoming an RA, and more! I don't think she can really fit all of these activities into her experience, but maybe I'm wrong?

Remember way back in the fall semester, when you may have been worried about all the free time your daughter had on her hands? You may be surprised how much a motivated, hard-working student like your daughter can fit into her schedule! Often the busiest college students can be the most productive and successful. Many students find that opportunities and responsibilities provide additional structure to their schedules, and, in turn, they find ways to use their time more effectively.

That said, your daughter may do best to choose her commitments strategically. She can make a list of all of the opportunities and experiences she is considering; she can then prioritize them and identify the ones that are most important to her. By doing this, she can also consider how much time each of the commitments will require of her, and whether any will conflict with one another. For example, if joining a sorority requires weekend engagements and being an RA may involve weekends on duty, how will she be able to do both? She may need to meet with the coordinators of these different campus experiences to make sure she has a clear picture.

Your daughter should also consider the long-term benefits of the activities she is interested in. Some of them may be more connected with her major than others; some may give her a chance to explore places she may like to live some day; some may allow her to develop skills she can use for the rest of her life. Your daughter's **academic advisor, the study**

abroad office and **the career center** may be able to help her understand these connections, and suggest when in her college career it may make more sense for her to try these opportunities.

What to expect of your ~~baby~~ young adult in this situation:

* She will make a list of the experiences in which she is most interested, and then will prioritize them in levels of importance to her.
* She will be realistic about her time commitments when making decisions
* She will meet with her academic advisor to discuss ways to incorporate these experiences into her years at college.
* She will meet with staff from appropriate offices to discuss the opportunities available to her.

STEP-BY-STEP . . .
STUDY ABROAD: PROVIDING YOUR ~~BABY~~ YOUNG ADULT WITH THE OPPORTUNITY TO SEE THE WORLD

Study abroad is a program that allows students to complete some of their academic credits in a university outside their country. These programs vary at different institutions, but often allow students to study at another university for a semester, a summer, or a full year while paying tuition through their home institution. There are study abroad programs throughout the world.

Universities that offer study abroad programs usually have a program coordinator or program office. These offices are usually called Study Abroad Office, Education Abroad Office, the Office of International Programs, or something similar. These offices can help students who are interested in studying abroad choose and apply for a program. They may also help students prepare for studying in a different country, provide support while they are abroad, and assist them in transitioning back to their home college.

Often, these programs have GPA requirements and do involve some advance planning of courses and credits, so it is helpful for students to plan ahead if they are considering studying abroad. An early visit to the study abroad office is recommended.

Step-By-Step . . .
Intramural Sports: Exercising Off the Baby Fat through Fun and Recreation

Many colleges and universities offer intramural sports. These recreational leagues of team sports are organized for students to participate in, and are a great outlet for fun exercise. The sports may be ones that many people have played in high school or in town leagues, such as soccer, volleyball and basketball. However, some universities have other offerings as well, including dodgeball, ultimate Frisbee, and Quidditch (a la Harry Potter). Most colleges allow students to form their own teams, made up of friends, roommates or classmates that play together for a season.

Universities that offer intramural sports typically have a staff or office that coordinates the teams and schedules. The intramural sports office is usually located in the athletic department or in the campus wellness center.

CHAPTER 10

May

● ● ●

Dear Mom and Dad,

I can't believe my first-year of college is almost over. Like everyone said way back in September, it really did go by sooooo fast. As I look back, I really do wish I had listened to you a little bit more--ya know, studied a bit harder and considered joining a club. Oh well............there's always sophomore year. I can't say I didn't have a blast though. I sure am going to miss all the new friends I made, but I am looking forward to seeing some of my high school squad. I hear some of the end of the year bashes are awesome. The upper class students say that NOTHING rivals the upcoming parties. I wish I didn't have so much to do though. I still have to study for finals and get a summer job. UGH. I guess I'll just hope for the best! Fingers crossed. See you at home soon.

Love,
Aidan

Growing Pains: What May Be Making Your ~~Baby~~ Young Adult Cranky This Month

- Preparing for and completing final exams and other projects
- Deciding on their living situation for the following academic year

- Increasing excitement about finishing the year and going home for the summer
- Looking for a job for the summer months
- Feeling sad to be leaving new friends or romantic relationships
- Feeling regret that their first year is over and they have not done as well as they expected, academically or socially

LEARNING DISABILITY DISCLOSURE

My daughter has a learning disability. Throughout high school, she received some extra support in her classes. However, when she went away to school, she decided to not disclose her disability and to try it on her own. My daughter has not done as well academically as she had hoped to this year, and now she is regretting not working with the college to get accommodations. Is it too late for her to succeed in college now?

What you are describing is very typical of first-years who have learning disabilities. Many times, after having a 504 plan/IEP all through high school and receiving extra assistance, students want to put that experience behind them and just "be like everyone else." Another common pattern for students with disabilities is that, by the time senior year of high school rolls around, they have developed compensatory skills, and find that they don't need to access accommodations as much as they did in their earlier high school years. College is a different ball game, however.

Most higher education curricula will challenge even the most pre-pared student. For students with learning challenges, the rigor of college compared to high school can potentially exacerbate the "symptoms" of a disability, so to speak. Even for those who have developed the most effective compensatory strategies, those strategies will not work to the same extent in a college environment. As a result, the best advice for a student going off to college with a learning disability is to submit documentation to the **access services** or **disability services office**. The next step would be to work with a professional staff member or learning specialist and seek approval for accommodations. Policies and procedures for going through the process of accommodations may vary depending on the institution, but not by much since institutions of higher education must adhere to federal guidelines.

Though your daughter decided to not seek out accommodations during her first year, it's definitely not too late. From here on out, she can follow through on the process of accommodations each semester and get the additional assistance she needs to be successful. She can also consider utilizing other **academic support services** such as advising or tutoring services to get her back on track.

What to expect of your ~~baby~~ young adult in this situation:

* She will talk to her academic advisor to discuss her academic progress this year, her plans for next semester, and to find out about disability services at her college.
* She will meet with someone in the disability services office to discuss her options for accessing services in the future.
* She will complete any necessary paperwork that the disability services office requires, which will likely include submitting appropriate documentation of her disability.
* She will meet with a learning specialist in future semesters to augment her coursework.

Commuting To College

My son's school is about 45 minutes away from our home. He lives on campus now, but has decided that he'd rather live at home next year. He says he made this decision in order to save money. However, I think he also found it difficult to live on campus, due to the partying culture at his school. He didn't really fit in. Will commuting to college ruin his college experience?

While the on-campus experience enables student to have a wide variety of interesting opportunities, campus life is not for everyone. Students choose to commute for a wide variety of reasons. Some students do so out of financial necessity, while others choose this option because they simply don't want to bear the expense of a residential experience. For them, it may be making a prudent decision to commute in an effort to prevent student loan debt upon graduation. Other students commute because they may need to work and continue to contribute to their family's income. For these students, they may still have other responsibilities at home like caring for an elderly family member or younger sibling.

There are myriad reasons for students choosing the commuter college experience over the residential experience. For your son, the campus culture was not the best fit for him at this stage and that's OK. Commuters, like residential students, just need to take responsibility and make the best of their college experience. He will continue to have access to the all of the same clubs and organizations, and all of the campus resources. He just may have to be a little more intentional about staying connected on campus, since he won't be living there.

What is ultimately most important for college students is to have a positive academic experience and carefully choose courses and out-of-class or co-curricular activities that contribute to their career goals. While the social life of college is important, academic and career development is even more important. On a final side note, sometimes first-year students are more likely to engage in the partying atmosphere on college campuses and then, after they transition and "grow up" a bit, the campus party culture settles down during sophomore year. This may be the case on your son's campus and he might want to explore that possibility with a trusted professional at his school.

Lastly, your son may want to investigate if there is some type of **commuter organization.** Most schools, particularly those with a high population of commuters, have developed programs and designed activities to serve this population of students. If he does become a commuter, joining such an organization will help him feel connected to and engaged in his campus community.

What to expect of your ~~baby~~ young adult in this situation:

* He will talk to you or someone at his institution such as an advisor or resident director about his experience of living on campus.

- He will engage you in an ongoing discussion of expectations and arrangements for his living at home next semester.
- He will look into opportunities for commuters to get involved at his college, including the commuter services office.

NEW LIVING ARRANGEMENTS

I just learned that my daughter and some friends have paid a deposit on an apartment near campus for next semester. I loved knowing that she was being at least somewhat supervised in the residence hall this year, and I worry about her safety next year.

What your daughter and her friends have planned is a typical path for many college students. The first step is living away from home in a residence hall, and the next step is to test young adulthood and the independence that goes along with it even further by renting an apartment. Who knows? In the future, she may ask to study abroad and her living situation will be in a dorm or apartment in another country! One step at a time, though.

It's understandable that you are concerned about her safety. There are a few things you can ask her to look into. For example, some college campuses have enough residential space for all first-years, and then after that, housing opportunities and situations are different for sophomores, juniors, and seniors. The apartment she rented could be in an area where other students from her institution also rent apartments; therefore, she will be surrounded by her peers. If this is the case, then the institution may work closely with the local community by partnering on a neighborhood crime watch, for example. You may also want to ask your daughter to contact the local police department in the area. Crime records are public and she could look into the relative safety of the neighborhood based on the last year's police records.

While you are right to be concerned about safety issues, there are also other issues to consider when moving into an apartment with peers. For instance, how will your daughter and her friends pay bills, share expenses, handle errands like grocery shopping and split up domestic chores? The list of responsibilities when living on your own in an apartment situation are many. The conflicts that arise living in an apartment are likely to be more complex than when she lived in a residence hall with just one roommate. Before she moves in with her friends, they may want to come up with a plan of action related to how they are going to handle all of the additional responsibilities of living on their own in an apartment, like creating chore charts, for example. While planning their approach to living together may seem like an obvious task to tackle, if they aren't proactive, they'll find themselves arguing about whose turn it is to take the garbage out.

Finally, she may want to consider how she will balance the new living situation with the responsibilities of her academics and coursework. Living in an apartment adds more to the "to-do" list. No longer if she's hungry will she be able to go grab a sandwich in the cafeteria or have a hot meal easily accessible. In order to make that happen in an apartment, planning ahead, shopping, preparing and cooking are in order. Is she ready for the additional responsibilities on top of managing her academic priorities?

What to expect of your ~~baby~~ young adult in this situation:

- She will do research and confirm with you that the selected apartment is in a safe location.
- She and her roommates will develop a plan to implement that considers their safety, including locking doors, walking from campus at night, and keeping one another informed of their whereabouts.
- She will talk with her roommates and you about the financial issues that typically arise when a student lives off campus, including rent payments, responsibility for utility bills, food shopping, etc.
- She will be sure to keep the lines of communication open with her apartment mates and create a strategy to resolve potential issues that arise.
- She will maintain the same academic standards that she did while living on campus.

Final Exam Stress

My son wants to make sure he finishes his first year by being on the dean's list. He is putting lots of pressure on himself to ace his finals. I'm concerned about his pulling all-nighters and non-stop studying. He is going to wear himself out.

You have just described what the majority of college students experience, not just first-years, during a midterm or final exam period, particularly the conscientious students. For conscientious students, putting pressure on themselves is fairly common. You can't blame him for wanting to finish off his first year of college successfully. Still, it's understandable that you are concerned. Undue stress and pressure can cause the immune system to be compromised and, as you said, he will get run down, and possibly sick. This is something you certainly will want to check in with him about.

The greater concern here is if he is pulling all-nighters. Almost every college student has pulled an all-nighter or two to study for a class here or there during their college careers, but it is certainly problematic if this is the primary study approach that he is applying across the board in all of his classes. If this is the case, then it's a pretty good indication that he did not keep up with his work throughout the semester and fell behind. If he procrastinated his studying, then perhaps the only way for him to pull himself out of the hole at this point is to stay up all night to jam all of his work in.

Non-stop studying is not the problem during a midterm or final exam period. That's exactly what a hard-working, diligent college student should be doing, with appropriate breaks built in, of course. The problem is *when* he is studying. That is, if the day time hours do not suffice and he needs to study through the night, he is likely not as prepared as he should be. Rest assured though, young adults are pretty resilient, and even if he is pulling all-nighters this time around, he will survive; however, next time around, he should plan ahead so that he thrives during the final exam period. Most study skills experts will say that preparing for finals begins on the first day of classes.

Your son should consider reaching out for support to insure that he has planned a balanced study schedule with periodic breaks. This would include being certain to maintain healthy eating and sleeping patterns and reaching out to his friends for support. He might also consider taking the next step by using professors' **office hours** and **the learning center** to supplement the studying he is doing on his own.

What to expect of your ~~baby~~ young adult in this situation:

* He will find out what activities and resources are available for students to blow off steam during finals week, and make an effort to relax for a period every day.
* He will create a study schedule will a balance of planned study time for each class and build in breaks.
* He will utilize academic resources like professors' office hours and tutoring services if needed.
* He will maintain healthy eating and sleeping habits as much as possible.
* He will seek out academically inclined friends to study with for additional support.

Summer Plans

I have been following my daughter's recent social media posts to her friends from home. They have already made plans for a beach week and a road trip, and they aren't even home from college yet! I want her to have a fun summer, but I think she is going to have a rude awakening when she gets home and realizes she has our house rules to follow.

You have pointed out yet another transition in your relationship with your daughter. First, she made the transition from high school to college--a big step. During her first year, she had a lot of freedom where she likely gained a great deal of independence and confidence from living on her own. While away, she only had herself (and perhaps her roommate) to answer to. The transition back home may be a bit challenging.

You will need to strike a healthy balance with your daughter as she returns to her home-life with you. On one hand, you want to honor her growth and her maturing into a young adult, and perhaps give her more freedoms than you did when she was living with you as a high school student. On the other hand, she will have to honor your house rules; it can't be "anything goes." You will have to come to some kind of compromise.

With freedom comes responsibility. She still has to be responsible to you, your family life, and your house rules; though, you may want to alter those rules so that they align more closely with the college student experience as opposed to a high school one. In engaging in the conversation to revise the house rules for a better fit, rather than leading the conversation, you may want to allow her to be part of the process, giving her a more equal role in determining the rules if she seems to be ready for that step. Let her be the one to come up with viable solutions to your new living experience together and negotiate the parameters from there.

What to expect of your ~~baby~~ young adult in this situation:

* She will engage in a dialogue with you regarding household expectations and responsibilities.
* She will follow your family's house rules.
* She will balance her fun summer activities with productive ones, like holding a job, volunteering or brushing up on academic skills.

SUMMER JOB

My husband and I expect our son to get a job this summer so that he has money for living expenses and books during sophomore year. Even though we have been nagging him since spring break to start looking, he hasn't found a job yet. Instead, he's been focused on finding an unpaid internship related to his major. We worry that he is not going to have enough cash to return to school in the fall.

The good news is that your son has been diligent in his efforts to find an internship connected to his major. That's likely advice he received from professors, the career center, or perhaps upper class peers. While it is sound advice, unfortunately, some academic internships are unpaid, yet for many majors, having an internship is an important component of building a resume in order to land a job in certain fields upon graduation. He may want to utilize the career center at his institution to find out whether paid internships are available for his major; then he can kill two birds with one stone. That is, he can earn money for his living expenses for next year and begin to build his resume at the same time. If he discovers that only unpaid internships are available, and if finances are the main concern, he may have to forego the internship this summer, and find a job that pays.

As your son is a first-year student, he still has plenty of time to figure out getting the requisite number of internships necessary for his major and sorting out how he will manage his expenses. He has at least three more winter breaks, and three more summers to focus on landing internships. Once he gets all the information he needs related to internships, his major, and expenses, he can think about some financial planning for the next three years so that he can cover his living expenses and begin to build a robust resume filled with relevant experiences. Before he leaves campus for the summer, he may find it helpful to speak with a staff member in the **career center** about his goals and options.

What to expect of your ~~baby~~ young adult in this situation:

- He will visit the career services office at his university to find out about paid and unpaid internship options, both during the summer and during the academic year.
- He will review his expenses from the previous year, and estimate the money he will need for the upcoming fall.
- He will develop a plan to earn the money he will need for the next academic year.

STEP-BY-STEP . . .
CAREER SERVICES: BEYOND YOUR ~~BABY'S~~ YOUNG ADULT'S FIRST PAPER ROUTE

Most universities have a career services office. This campus resource assists students in a variety of ways related to choosing and finding a career. Typical services provided include career exploration workshops, internship opportunities, resume writing guidance, interview skill development and job/career fairs. Some of these offices also help students with graduate school decisions.

Many students assume career services offices primarily work with graduating seniors, but this is not accurate. First-year students can benefit from visiting the career services office, especially if they are trying to decide on a major, are interested in finding an internship, or want to learn more about a particular career field. Career services offices provide targeted programming for all four years of a student's college experience. You may also find that some career services offices can even help with a summer job or summer internships.

STEP-BY-STEP . . .
LEARNING DISABILITY SERVICES: HELPING YOUR ~~BABY~~ YOUNG ADULT GAIN ACCESS TO A POSITIVE EDUCATIONAL EXPERIENCE

The Americans with Disabilities Act (ADA) requires that college and universities must provide services for learning disabled students. These services are typically provided through the disability or access services office. While these offices are housed in different areas and go by a variety of names, depending on the institution, if a student has a learning disability, this is where they should go to find out about services and accommodations.

Students with learning disabilities may be allowed accommodations for their courses, based on documentation of a disability. In addition, disability services offices may offer students workshops, learning specialists, and other resources to help them succeed with their academics. Further, if a student suspects that they may have a previously undiagnosed learning disability, the disability services office can help educate them on processes and procedures necessary for accessing services.

STEP-BY-STEP . . .
COMMUTER SERVICES: WHEN YOUR ~~BABY~~ YOUNG ADULT NO LONGER NEEDS A CAR SEAT

Many universities and colleges have a commuter services department. This office may be called The Commuter Office, The Commuter Connection, or Commuter Student Services. Commuter services usually provide a space on campus expressly set aside for commuters, with resources such as lockers, a refrigerator, ride-sharing boards, and a space to gather when not in class. This helps commuter students feel more at home on campus, and allows them to meet one another.

At some universities, commuter services have professional staff members that help commuters to integrate into campus life. They may offer social events and other activities especially for commuters.

Students who are commuting or planning to commute should visit the office and talk to a professional staff member and other commuters to learn more about the campus life for commuter students.

For more advice for parents of college students and the higher education experi-ence, visit collegereadyparent.org.

REFERENCES

Addiction Center (2016). *Greek life and substance abuse.* Retrieved from https://www.addictioncenter.com/college/drinking-drug-abuse-greek-life/

Anderson, D.S., & Gadaleto, A. (2001). *Results of the 2000 College Alcohol Survey.* Fairfax, VA: Center for the Advancement of Public Health, George Mason University.

Barry, A. E. (2007). Using theory-based constructs to explore the impact of Greek membership on alcohol-related beliefs and behaviors: A systematic literature review. *Journal of American College Health, 56,* 307–315. doi:10.3200/JACH.56.3.307-316

Boyer, E.L. (1987). *College: The undergraduate experience in America.* New York: Harper & Row.

College Parents of America. (2007, March 14). *Second Annual National Survey on College Parent Experiences.* Retrieved from www.collegeparents.org.

Counseling Services-Bryant University. (2016). *Counseling services.* Retrieved from http://www.bryant.edu/student-life/campus-services/counseling-services.htm

Cuseo, J.B. (2003). Comprehensive academic support for student during the first year of college. In G.L. Kramer & Associates, *Student academic services: an integrated approach* (pp. 271-301). San Francisco: Jossey-Bass.

DiPrete, J. (2005). *The well student.* [pamphlet]. Used with permission.

Hazard, L. L., & Nadeau, J.P. (2012). *Foundations for learning.* Boston: Pearson.

Hood, A.B., Craig, A.F., & Ferguson, B.W. (1992, September). The impact of athletics, part-time employment and other activities on academic achievement. *Journal of College Student Development, 33,* 447-453.

Hyman, J.S., & Jacobs, L.F. (2009, August 12). Why does diversity matter at college anyway? *US News and World Report.* Retrieved from http://www.usnews.com/education/blogs/professors-guide/2009/08/12/why-does-diversity-matter-at-college-anyway

Light, R.J. (2001). *Making the most of college: Students speak their minds.* Cambridge, MA: Harvard University Press.

Matt, G.E., Pechersky, B., & Cervantes, C. (1991). High school study habits and early college achievement. *Psychological Reports, 69,* 91-96.

Mayo Clinic. (2016). *Diseases and conditions: colic.* Retrieved from http://www.mayoclinic.org/diseases-conditions/colic/basics/definition/con-20019091

Perozzi, B., Rainey, A., and Wahlquist, Z. (2003). A review of the effects of student employment on academic achievement. *The Bulletin Online: The Bimonthly Magazine of the Association of College Unions International, 71,* 15-20.

Pope, J. (2005, August 28). Colleges try to deal with hovering parents. *USAToday.*

Shellenbarger, S. (2005, July 28). Tucking the kids in – in the dorm: colleges ward off overinvolved parents. *Wall Street Journal,* p.D1.

Van de Water, G. (1996). The effect of part-time work on academic performance and progress: An examination of the Washington state work-study program. In Kincaid, R. (Ed.), *Student employment: Linking college and the workplace.* South Carolina University: National Resource Center for the Freshman Year Experience and Students in Transition, 57-67.

Made in the USA
Middletown, DE
05 May 2017